There are tim...
to keep our ears, e...
what musician Da... *cuus 'Whoever, Whatever.'*
That would be every day. The veteran performer whose
signature sound comes from the double flute, now gives
voice to the inspiration and life lessons that he has gleaned
from three decades on the road.

Divine Inner Guidance *(DIG) is the perfect title for*
this book since it really IS about digging into the rich soil
of experience and coming away with precious treasures.
He weaves tales about fellow musicians including Bob
Dylan and Paul McCartney.

This book can be your key to opening the door to your
deepest dreams and heart's desires. Listen to them. Trust
them.

—Edie Weinstein, journalist,
motivational speaker and
author of *The Bliss Mistress*
Guide To Transforming the
Ordinary Into the Extraordinary

You have an amazing talent and world view. That
came through loud and clear, especially showing the
value of asking for Divine Guidance no matter what the
situation. That really is the reason to write this book.
Highly authentic.

—Barbara McNichol,
Author of Word Trippers

I'm an avid reader, and many books don't hold my attention. However, David Young's Divine Inner Guidance *kept me up until the wee hours of the morning. I couldn't put it down! I loved his fascinating and fun stories, heartfelt messages, and the truly divine inspiration that he shares with the reader. It's personal and poignant. You're with David every step of the way, urging him on, feeling his pain, celebrating his successes, and wishing you were there with him sharing his incredible journey.*

ENJOY and savor this great book!

—Susan Duval,
Susan Duval Seminars

Divine Inner Guidance

Your Intuition Can
Transform Your Life

David Young

Also by David Young:

Village of Dreams

Divine Inner Guidance

Your Intuition Can
Transform Your Life

David Young

Young, David 1962-
Divine Inner Guidance: Your Intuition Can Transform Your Life / by David
Young p. cm.
ISBN 9781478218364

Book cover and interior design by Doug Munson
Cover photo by Zarek

Bulk purchase discounts, for educational purposes, are available. Contact
the publisher for more information.

First edition

David Young Music
1464 Lake Dr. West
Chanhassen, MN 55317
www.davidyoungmusic.com

Table of Contents

For some reason some of us, have had lives that have been gigantic adventures—failures, successes, far reaching travel, many loves, many relationships, loneliness, and hearing God's voice.

Paul McCartney kept reaching his head up to see over everyone else, trying to figure out how I was doing what I was doing and smiling at me the whole time.

I didn't always have it down, spiritually. It was a process. I actually began my quest for understanding more about my intuition and spirituality in an AC/DC tribute band in the 1980s.

From what I've seen, success comes to people who are willing to do what no one else is willing to do. The AC/DC tribute band was an amazing experience of survival in many ways.

Preface

$\mathcal{E}$arly on, I learned to trust Divine Inner Guidance, something we all have. When I listened to it, remarkable direction was given that made my life better, richer, and easier. Things magically seemed to "fall in place." When I didn't listen to it, I paid dearly, as you will read. Divine Inner Guidance is trying to make our life more enjoyable. You could say some of these lessons have been my karma, yet some people say there is no such thing as karma. In my opinion, everything we do creates a reaction and an experience that either brings us something enjoyable or something not enjoyable. So, there's enjoyable karma and not enjoyable karma. When we listen and tune in, our life is more enjoyable. It's that simple.

I often compare my own spiritual life of learning, from listening to God's guidance to the life of a teenager.

Let's say that by the time a child gets to be a teenager, he is halfway to being an adult. He knows a lot more than when he was a baby, and at times he might even think that he knows it all. A parent has twenty or thirty more years of life, mistakes, and valuable experience to offer the teenager. Most of the time, the desires of the teenager are pulling him this way and that, and valuable advice is ignored, forgotten, or overlooked. After a certain amount of failure and painful experience, the hard knocks of life soften up the kid and humble him, so he is finally open to hearing something that could make his life easier again. God waits for us to listen to the Divine Inner Guidance, just like a parent waits for the teenager to wake up and accept the help and guidance that is priceless and always there. If it were all that easy . . .

Listening to Intuition

Some people's lives have been a straight line, without many twists and turns. When we look back on them, there aren't many high and low points, dramas, or obstacles they overcame. Let's compare them to a wheat cracker for a moment—mild, four lines leading to four corners, one color, one flavor, and cut and dried.

But some of us, for some reason, have had lives that have been gigantic adventures—failures, successes, far reaching travel, many loves, many relationships, loneliness, and hearing God's voice after believing it didn't exist. Mistakes have been made, lessons hopefully learned, and many obstacles overcome. Let's compare these experiences to a bowl of spicy spaghetti, twisting and turning with colored vegetables and exotic meats strewn on top, each bite an adventure.

I had enough stories to fill a large book fifteen

years ago, and all of the things that have happened since could probably fill two more. My friends and family call them "David stories." The coincidences are sometimes hard to fathom. Watching the hand of Spirit lead me from disaster to miracles has made my life an amazing journey.

I've thought about writing this numerous times, but perhaps because of the movies I have made, the musicals I have written, and all the albums I have produced, I haven't gotten around to it. Maybe now, because I'm getting older and there is value in these stories that people enjoy, I decided to finally start compiling them in this book. After reliving all this in the process, I feel proud and kind of surprised—that I'm still here, still doing what I love to do as an artist.

Most people say that they wouldn't change a thing if they could go back and do it all again. I definitely would, but then I wouldn't have written this book.

2

From My Hand to His Hand

Over the years, many cancer hospitals, hospice workers, and therapists of all kinds have used my music to help suffering patients and families deal with difficulties they face in their lives.

One of the saddest news stories of 1999 was that Linda McCartney, Paul McCartney's wife, was dying of breast cancer. Many hearts around the world went out to Paul when his wife passed away.

I always had a great appreciation for Paul, and I wondered how I could get some of my music to him. Despite the fact that he's very famous, he's still a human being, and peaceful, relaxing music could help him heal through his grieving process.

I had a lot of contacts in the music and entertainment business when I was living in Los Angeles, but no one I knew at the time had a connection with Paul McCartney. A few months of dead-end phone calls later, I let go of the idea of finding him. I just surrendered it to Spirit.

Inwardly, I said to myself, "God, I put this into your hands. If it is meant for Paul to have some of my music to help him heal, then may the blessings be." I imagined this thought being lifted up from my hands, sailing up to the sky and out to the heavens.

I forgot about it and life went on.

Six months later, I got a call from the Atlanta Wholesale Gift Show. I was scheduled to have a booth at the show in January to sell my music, and they were asking how much I'd charge to perform at a corporate event connected to the gift show. I quoted her a price, and the woman on the phone said my price was more than what they wanted to pay.

Then we spoke about the arrangements for my booth at the gift show; the location, table and chairs, electricity, etc. As she continued to fill me in on the technical information, I had this nagging feeling to ask her who the corporate event was for. This was unusual. Normally, after you give someone a quote, the conversation is over if it's not in the budget. But I asked anyway, following the nudge of Divine Inner Guidance.

"Heather McCartney, Paul McCartney's daughter," she said.

"Is Paul McCartney going to be there?" I couldn't stop myself from asking.

"I'm really not sure," she answered.

"When is the event?" I queried.

"It's the night before the gift show starts," she replied. I was booked for the show anyway, and I only had to get there one night earlier.

"What is your budget for music at the event?" I asked her.

She told me her budget, I thought about it, then said, "I'll do it."

My wife and I went to the airport the next day and had the tickets changed. When I told them why I was changing the flight dates, they waived the change fee and wished me good luck.

We flew to Atlanta for the gigantic gift show that filled three buildings downtown. The McCartney organization had a large showroom on one of the higher floors, displaying all of Heather's designs: plates, rugs, and various gift items with a Southwestern flair. When Heather was a child, her family spent summer vacations outside Tucson, Arizona. She was influenced by the colorful styles of the local artisans there.

I was to play music inside the main entrance of the showroom at the event. The press conference and her artwork were in the room across from me. People crowded the halls, causing quite a huge buzz in the building.

From where I was standing, I could see Paul, Heather, and their bodyguard through the large showroom windows. They started walking down the hall past the other showrooms toward me. I'd never seen so many women in their forties, fifties, and sixties losing it as if they were teenage girls!

When they finally got to the doorway, Paul pointed to me and said to Heather, "Hey look, the flute guy is here." They both waved to me as if we were all old friends. That was surreal. The event coordinator must have sent them one of my CDs in advance.

The press was all over them immediately, cameras and microphones in the air, firing a flurry of questions at them, trying for an interview. This was Paul's first public appearance since Linda had passed away six months earlier, and every major TV network, news-paper, and magazine were there. Another day in the life of a Beatle, but this was a little different. He had adopted Heather when she was three years old, and he was there to support her.

The funny thing was that Paul seemed to be very interested and amused that I was playing two flutes at one time in harmony. His entourage attempted to get them through to the press room for approximately fif-teen minutes, all the time right in front of where I was playing. Paul kept reaching his head up to see over everyone else, trying to figure out how I was doing what I was doing and smiling at me the whole time. Eventually they did make it over to the other side where the press conference was to be held.

My mind still reeled from the friendly vibes I got from Paul and Heather. They made me feel like I was one of them, part of their entourage. The family videographer kept smiling and coming over to film me a number of times.

One young guy in his twenties wearing a surfer beanie really stuck out in the 45- to 75-year-old crowd at the event. I wondered what he was doing there, but most of all I was wondering why he kept hitting on my wife. (I'm not a jealous guy, but apparently he wasn't aware that she was with me.) He would also chat with the family videographer each time he came by to film me, so I finally realized that this was Heather's brother, James.

I decided to ask my wife to get me one of my CDs so I could sign it and give it to James as a gift for Heather. (That would also give him a second to realize that he'd been hitting on my wife.) I signed the cover of the CD "To Heather, Best of luck, David Young." After James saw me kiss my wife and get the CD from her, he disappeared. I didn't see him again for the remainder of the event.

Eventually the press conference ended and mania followed Paul and Heather back across the room as they were trying to leave. The best way I can describe what I saw was a swarm of bees buzzing around a nest. People were flipping out trying to get Paul's autograph. Sounds of hysteria and excitement filled the air. The entourage had to cross to my side of the room once again to exit the main door. It struck me that we were likely going to get one last chance to make eye contact and say goodbye. Nothing in Paul's life happens quickly, just getting across the room took twenty minutes.

Finally there they were, right in front of me. Paul suddenly stopped to talk to me and quieted down the whole crowd. The room was instantly silent.

He looked at me, smiled, and said, "Very well done."

"Thank you very much, Sir," I replied.

Time stood still. I'd called him "Sir" out of respect for him as a musician. He had just been knighted and seemed surprised to have an American call him "Sir." He wore a curious look on his face.

"This was extremely well done, and you're not getting the praise you so deserve," he said. He then started clapping for me. The whole crowd joined in, figuring that since Paul McCartney has pretty good taste in music, they better clap for me, too. Everyone was happy and proud that Paul took the time to honor me. I felt ten feet tall.

I remembered then that I'd signed a CD to give to Heather's brother, but since he'd disappeared, I still had it. I reached over, picked it up and handed it to Paul. When he saw that it was signed, "To Heather, Best of Luck, David Young," he gave me a curious look—as if I'd just performed a magic trick. I could practically read his thoughts. *How did he come up with a personally signed CD without me seeing him sign it?*

After a moment I said, "This is for Heather because it's her special day." He was very happy that I put the spotlight back on her and he strongly shook my hand. Then they left. No one looked at me the same after that.

Once the event was over, Paul's manager approached me and said, "I can't tell you how many times Paul remarked on how much he liked your music. He truly thought it was great." Knowing the style of Heather's art, I had chosen all songs with a Native American flavor.

"I enjoyed your music, too," the manager continued, "and if you could give me a CD for myself, I'd also be happy to give one to Paul."

I've told this story many times, but it wasn't until a year later that I remembered my first intention was to give Paul one of my CDs for healing when his wife Linda had passed away. And even though I wasn't able to find anyone to get my music to Paul McCartney, Spirit found a way for me to give my music to him directly—from my hand to his hand.

To download David's enchanting version of "Let It Be," either capture the QR code with your mobile device or enter **http://tinyurl.com/7lk7dn3** in your browser.

3

Changing Our World by Changing
the Way We Think

I once attended a wonderful quantum physics workshop with Dr. Joe Dispenza. He taught the value of choosing our thoughts carefully, because this is what creates our world. Our outer world is a manifestation of our inner thoughts. I got to experience this first-hand in 1982 with my band QT Hush in Syracuse, New York.

I didn't always have it down, spiritually. It was a process. It was actually this band which sparked my quest for understanding more about my intuition and spirituality.

The story begins just before our manager had the brilliant idea for us to become an AC/DC tribute band. We had been a run-of-the-mill hard rock band going nowhere. To make matters worse, the band, originally called Outakontrol, was thousands of dollars in debt when I joined, so most of the money from our gigs went to pay back the debt.

I was surviving on CARE packages of canned food and microwave popcorn that my mom sent me. When I'd quit college to join the band, my dad stopped supporting me financially. I was willing to starve to play my music. After the canned food was gone, I lived on popcorn and ketchup, and when I ran out of ketchup I ate popcorn with mustard.

We were a five-piece band consisting of a lead singer, bass player, and a drummer; John McKenna and I both played lead guitar. If you've ever seen the mockumentary Spinal Tap, this is what our personalities were really like.

To give you an insight into the mind of a lead guitarist, here's a little joke. It's too true, which was part of our problem.

How many guitar players does it take to screw in a light bulb?

Answer: Ten. The first one screws in the light bulb and the other nine all say, "I could have done that much better."

John and I really hated each other because we were both competing for the same spotlight. After a bad rehearsal I remember wondering, "How can I ever survive this situation?" Then I had an evil idea that actually taught me something about quantum physics.

I decided I would trick John by making him think that all of a sudden I actually liked him. At first he didn't trust it, but every time we were together, I'd put on an act that he was my best friend. After doing this for awhile , I forgot it was an act. I'd gotten so used to acting like he was my best friend that he actually became my best friend! When I changed the way I was thinking about him, the universe around me changed as well.

The financial situation with the band, however, was still precarious. The country was in a recession at that time. Money was tight everywhere, and the gas crisis was making it worse.

It had gotten to the point where Randy, our manager, called us together for a meeting one day. "Look guys," he said, "I'm having a hard time sleeping at night because you guys are still starving. I have one last thing for you to try. If you're not willing to try it, our working relationship is over."

For the record, many a musician has been through this trial-by-fire before they made it. I read that Frank Sinatra was homeless before he was successful. Jethro Tull lived in the basement of a bombed out building in England and survived on a sack of potatoes for a month. The first Jeff Beck/Rod Stewart concert tour of the US was cancelled after five weeks because their band was starving to death. Once again, the people who "did what no one else was willing to do" became the champions at the top of their field.

Back in 1980, AC/DC was the most popular band

in the world with their album Back in Black. Randy's idea was that we should become an AC/DC tribute band. Bear in mind that this was before the concept of tribute bands had become popular. It was out-of-the-box thinking on his part. He only knew of one other tribute band. They were a Rolling Stones tribute band from Canada called the Blushing Brides, and they were making $20,000 a night!

John, the other lead guitarist, had a voice that sounded just like Brian Johnson, AC/DC's lead singer. Every time we played AC/DC, the crowd would go crazy. So, John went from being the other lead guitarist to lead singer. Donny, who had been our lead singer, became the bass player. He'd never played bass before, so I taught him the eight notes he needed to play AC/DC during our five weeks of rehearsal. Our bass player, Tom, became the rhythm guitarist. He already knew how to play four of the six strings, anyway. I became the only lead guitarist and had to dress up like Angus Young in the shorts and the blue suit. My job was to run all over the stage non-stop while we played the ninety minute show each night. I was a hyper-active kid anyway, so this was a perfect fit.

Our drummer quit because he wasn't going to play in a band with guys who'd never played their instruments before. (Typical musician mentality, thinking it was all about musicianship.) We couldn't find a professional drummer to play with us for that reason, so we had no choice but to let Bernie, our sound engineer, become the drummer. Bernie gained his experience in a drum and bugle corps, but he hadn't played drums since seventh grade.

Bottom line, what we lacked in ability we made up for in energy and attitude. Eventually we became the second highest-grossing band on the circuit behind the Blushing Brides.

I came up with this saying, "If you think like a musician, you're going to starve like a musician."

If you approach your career like everyone else in your field, you'll have the same limitations as everyone else in your field.

Think outside the box. Outside the box, you get the chance to excel.

4

Survival is a Great Teacher

*F*rom what I've seen, success comes to people who are willing to do what no one else is willing to do.

The AC/DC tribute band was an amazing experience of survival in many ways. We lived on five dollars a day. The five members of the band plus our three-man road crew, had to share one hotel room when we started touring—that was all we could afford.

We'd take the box springs off the two mattresses and two of us would sleep on each them. That took care of eight of us, but if our manager was traveling with us, one of us had to sleep in the bathtub. The biggest challenge was getting towels for eight or nine people without the hotel finding out.

Eventually, after a lot of hard, tireless work, we became one of the most popular touring groups on the East Coast. Clubs would sometimes cancel national acts with songs on the radio if we needed a gig to fill our schedule.

But after awhile I got bored traveling in the band with the other guys. Sometimes I made friends at gigs and decided to hang with them afterwards. I'd crash at their place and tell the band I would hitchhike to meet them in the next city on the tour. Our routing usually allowed us three hours between each gig, but some were as far as seven hours away.

An opening band always played before us at the clubs. We'd go on at midnight, allowing me plenty of time to wake up, shower, have something to eat, and get to the highway to hitch. I never missed a gig.

I learned something that I called the "hitchhiking technique." I later used it in other areas of my life. When hitchhiking, you have a choice to either stand there on the side of the road, or walk with your thumb out. If I was taking little steps toward where I wanted to go, at least I felt I was getting closer to where I wanted to be—even if it was far away.

The whole Venice Beach approach was exactly that. We'd play and sell CDs on our own, one by one, a little step at a time. I sold over 1,000,000 albums with that approach. Back in 1991, very few groups did that. For a rock band to put out their own album wasn't cool because that meant no record companies wanted you.

While in Los Angeles, I became friends with a woman named Yosha. She was married to Kenny Gradney, a member of Little Feat. Yosha and I met while I was performing in the Shakespearean play

Twelfth Night. We'd have sushi once in awhile, and she'd often say, "Tell Kenny about how you started selling your tapes and CDs down at Venice Beach and how, in just a few years of traveling to art festivals, you sold 100,000 copies."

So I spoke to him, recommending that his band start making their own albums and selling them at their live shows. But that was way below them. They were world-famous, and that's not what world-famous bands did back then.

Five years passed, and since both of us were traveling so much, I hadn't seen Kenny at all. Then we both suddenly found ourselves back in Los Angeles at the same time. We met for dinner.

"How are you doing?" I asked him

"Life is great," he said. "We started making our own CDs and selling them at our shows. We've tripled our income!" He'd forgotten our conversations from years before, but I was happy for him.

Another guitar player friend I'd met in Los Angeles back then was Steve Caton. Steve lived in Venice when he wasn't touring with Tori Amos. He told me, "You have the best gig in L.A. at Venice Beach, you know that? You don't have to travel anywhere and you get to sleep in your own bed every night."

Whenever his friends from out of town visited, he'd always bring them down to the beach to watch us. It was hard to believe that as a street performer I was admired by a famous touring musician. We tend to think the grass is always greener.

Waiting for a knight in shining armor to come along and sweep you up to the top is a common fairytale in entertainment and the performing arts. Taking your career into your own hands instead is more often the only thing we can do.

Yanni had played at Venice Beach for a few years before his career took off. Cirque de Soleil started out performing on the streets in Montreal. Colonel Sanders, the man who started Kentucky Fried Chicken, got his start by going door to door with his products.

There's a saying that, "God helps those who help themselves."

Before I became successful in music, I was a heating and air conditioning salesman. I needed a job because my wife was pregnant at the time, and I wasn't making much money in music.

I responded to a newspaper ad. When the manager picked up the phone, she asked me, "How much experience have you had selling furnaces?"

I answered, "None, but I'm from New York and I can sell anything."

"That's the kind of person I'm looking for," she responded. During the job interview, she confided in me, "When I was hired for this manager's job, the reason I was hired was because I said the same thing!" She had no previous experience selling HVAC, but now she had fifteen salesmen working under her.

During the training, we were asked the most basic question, "What is the difference between a furnace and a boiler?" I was actually laughed at because I didn't know. That was incentive, though. I became the top salesman in the company. (By the way—a furnace blows hot air and a boiler heats with hot water.)

We often got leads from our main office, but when there were no leads, there was nothing to do. I'm not comfortable doing nothing, so I went out walking through the neighborhoods, going door-to-door and offering a free estimate for a new furnace or A/C unit. That also gave me extra practice selling, or trying to sell.

On one occasion, after I rang the doorbell, a woman answered the door saying, "Wow, you're fast. I just hung up the phone from calling for an estimate. My furnace just stopped working."

You could say that was luck. I call it Divine Inner Guidance putting me in the right place at the right time. But, you see, I was also willing to do what none of the other salesmen were willing to do.

I have to say that the most successful people I've met in the music industry were definitely not the most talented with their instruments. Very often, very talented people have egos built up from getting lots of praise. They think their talent is going to make them famous.

Hanging in there, being creative, doing what no one else is willing to do, and putting yourself out there is much more important.

I have a saying about this: "Survival is a great teacher."

When we played at Venice Beach, there were some songs that would draw people and prompt them to reach into their pockets to buy a tape, or later, a CD. I could get rid of a crowd in seconds if I started to play a lot of fast notes and show off. The audience seemed to act more favorable to long, beautiful notes that were peaceful. By seeing what people liked and responding to that, I was able to make a living from my music.

5

I'm the Window Man

eople who only know me as "the flute man" find it very difficult to imagine me in a blue suit jacket, baseball cap, and shorts playing lead guitar. But it's true. From 1980-82, I dressed up as lead guitarist, Angus Young, in an AC/DC tribute band called QT Hush.

We were billed as the loudest band around. That was my fault. At the time Deep Purple was in the Guinness Book of World Records for playing the loudest concert ever. I was using the same equipment built by their sound guy, John Dawk, to play in clubs. My guitar by itself was louder than three complete bands playing together nowadays.

Playing in a rock band doing one-nighters all over the country was tiring, monotonous work, to say the least. We had our one full meal each day at Denny's, McDonald's, or Burger King. They were our home away from home. The clubs usually gave us something like pretzels or peanuts to snack on at night when we arrived for sound check. Pizza was a real bonus. My nutrition was so bad that my skin started to change to a shade of green.

Animal House had just come out and featured John Belushi instigating the now-famous food fight scene. I hadn't learned anything about karma yet, so for kicks I started food fights with the band all over the country. It's not anything I'm proud of now, but I threw stuff at the windows and all over the place, generally just making a mess.

My time with QT Hush came to an end when I met the woman who became my first wife. It was time to quit the band to do something more original. However, while we were rehearsing to get a new show ready, I needed to find a job to support myself.

For three months no one would hire me. I think looking like a caveman with hair down to my waist had something to do with it.

I saw an ad in the newspaper for a janitor, and after a short phone interview, the man said, "Why don't you meet me at the Burger King in town at noon."

I arrived on time and after speaking with him for fifteen minutes he said, "I think you're intelligent enough to work for me as a janitor."

"Thanks," I said, "What does it pay?"

"Minimum wage," he replied.

"What are the hours?" I asked.

"Midnight to six in the morning," he answered.

"Which days of the week?" I asked.

"Only Friday and Saturday nights," he replied.

"Why the strange hours and only on weekends?" I asked.

Listen to this. Here's his reply, "Every weekend we have kids come in here wasted. They start food fights and throw crap all over the windows. I need someone to clean up the mess!"

I was so dense at the time I didn't realize that life was trying to teach me something about the karma I created. It wasn't until a year or so later as I was telling this story to a high school friend, that I finally connected the dots. I wrote a song about it. It never became famous, but it's called "I'm a Window Man, That's What I Am."

Another thing. To this day, after cleaning out the pickle barrels in that Burger King, I cannot stand the smell of pickles.

6

Try To Quiet Your Mind

Sometimes the hardest thing to do in life is to calm our minds. Our best chance for a moment of inner peace is often when we first wake up, before the engine of our mind starts running around planning our day. Finding a way to get our mind to settle down can be challenging, but it is a worthwhile effort.

Have you ever been out on a lake early in the morning when it's quiet and still, and then you look down at the water? You can see yourself perfectly. But if there are waves rolling across the water, you can't see anything except the waves. When our mind is racing, we can't hear anything else but that. When our mind is calm, we're more receptive. We're in a place where we're better able to hear our Divine Inner Guidance.

You can't listen to two radio stations at one time and get anything of value from it. When Divine Inner Guidance is giving us a message or a nudge, exercising a little self control to create stillness will give us a better chance of hearing it—instead of our mind chatter.

Try this technique: See how long you can go without thinking anything.

In the beginning you may have a hard time getting past five seconds, but the longer you can create stillness inside, the more you are going to be able to hear your own Divine Inner Guidance when you least expect it.

Give Yourself a Break:
A Quick, Easy, and Effective Technique

Give yourself a five minute mental break to just quiet down your mind during your day, and try not to think about anything.

Do you have any employees? Do you ask them to work eight hours straight without a break? No way.

Everyone needs a break.

7

I'm Not Afraid of Heaven

*S*ometimes when Divine Inner Guidance speaks to us, it is subtle, like a gentle nudge or a quiet voice. Sometimes it comes as a feeling. And sometimes it's really loud, in your face and obvious.

In 1990 I left Minneapolis to drive to California to give myself one last shot at a music career. I was going to be passing through Des Moines, Iowa, so I called my friend Ricky to tell him I'd like stop and see him on my way. He was delighted.

Ricky was the bass player in one of my bands. A super nice guy and great musician, he started complaining of terrible headaches. When he went to get checked out, he was diagnosed with a brain tumor. They only gave him six months to live after his chemo, so he moved from Minneapolis to Des Moines to spend the rest of his days with his mom. Des Moines is a three hour drive south from the Twin Cities, so as I drove I had plenty of time to ponder what the visit would be like. I had never experienced the loss of one of my friends.

When I got to his mom's trailer park, Ricky was full of smiles. The only way I could tell anything was wrong with his health was that his long rock 'n roll hair had thinned out all the way around. He wore a hat to cover that up, so he still looked as cool as ever. His spirit was still the same.

I was only going to stay one night and then continue the long drive to the West Coast. But we had so much fun hanging out together, I decided to stay two more nights. It made him really happy having me there. It just felt right and we had plenty of time to talk about everything.

"Are you afraid?" I asked him.

"Not at all," he said. "Every afternoon since I started the chemo, I take a nap and wake up in the same place, and I am with the same people in my 'dream world.' My teacher there is always the same, and after a few months I realized that this is the next world I'm going to when my body finally stops working here on earth.

"So, no, I'm not afraid because I know my life will continue, just in a different place with new friends."

The following day I left, and within an hour, a giant snowstorm hit the area. Because I'd listened to my Divine Inner Guidance, I got to spend extra time with my friend and still was protected on my journey.

8

Jackass Café

*N*ormally when people go to self-help seminars, it's positive and uplifting. Looking-at-the-bright-side stuff helps people recharge spiritually so they can find new ways to deal with the difficulties of the physical world. I love these seminars. Who doesn't?

Can you imagine being in the audience at one of these and hearing the speaker ask, "Who would like to stand up and share a story about the biggest blunder of your life?" (I can't imagine that either.)

From learning to listen to Divine Inner Guidance, I've had countless experiences where Spirit guided me and helped make my life better. It's incredible what happens when we listen to It. Parking spaces appear; we meet old friends we haven't seen in years—in the most bizarre places—and other wonderful things. Sometimes we can save ourselves huge amounts of unnecessary karma and stress by listening to It. It's also incredible what happens when we don't.

It takes wisdom and humility to learn the art of tuning in to Divine Inner Guidance.

So where does this wisdom come from?

Wisdom comes from experience.

How do we gain experience? We gain experience from making good decisions.

And how do we learn to make good decisions? Sometimes by first making bad decisions and then learning from them.

After I left Ricky's house, I headed west toward California. It was December.

An hour later he called me. A giant snowstorm hit just after I left. It missed me because I left at the perfect time. This kind of thing continued for the next couple of days as I drove, and two more times I was spared more dangerous driving in blizzards. I was centered and tuned in. Every decision I made seemed to be divinely guided.

The interesting thing about life, and the way our minds and egos work, is that it's natural for us to forget why things go so well sometimes.

Things go well because we're tuned in to our Divine Inner Guidance and are taking Its advice. Then we are guided by Spirit to do the right thing and be in the right place at the perfect time. (. . . and also not to be in the wrong place at the wrong time.)

As I drove through Arizona, I checked the map. I could see that the main highway would take me at least an hour west, then I'd have to change roads and drive an hour south to get to Flagstaff. I could also see a little road running diagonally between where I was and Flagstaff that appeared would save me at least an hour. It looked like a shortcut.

I will share with you what I've learned about shortcuts.

You can always recognize a shortcut because it takes you three times longer!

So I glanced over at the map thinking, *That little diagonal road would save me over an hour of driving.* My Divine Inner Guidance said, "Don't do it."

I continued on and realized I needed gas, so I pulled over at a little roadside gas station to fill up. There was a little grey-haired lady inside. I showed her my map, telling her my idea of taking the diagonal shortcut across, and pointing to the little road.

She sternly said, "Don't do it." Her tone and energy was so similar to the energy from my Divine Inner Guidance fifteen minutes earlier, that it actually felt strange.

A unique thing about common sense is that sometimes it conflicts with God's guidance. Common sense comes from the mind and previous experiences. God's guidance comes from far above the mental arena and has millions of years more experience than we have.

My mind jumped in and I told her, "But look how much shorter this route is. It has to save me at least ninety miles!" Again she said, "Don't do it!" and walked away.

I got back in my car wondering what I should do as I continued driving. Everything had been going so perfectly. I had sidestepped three snowstorms like magic and felt like I could do no wrong.

What's the worst thing that could happen? I thought. (It should be a gigantic sign when you ask yourself that question.)

The exit for my shortcut was approaching, and I went back and forth in my mind, *Should I or shouldn't I?*

My spirit of adventure urged me to go for it. (My guess is that you're probably calling my "spirit of adventure" something else right now. It's OK, so am I.)

As I sharply turned the steering wheel to exit off the highway at Exit 88, the gallon water jug on top of my suitcase in the passenger seat came flying over and hit me on my head.

I followed this road for a few miles until a sign ahead informed me that I was about to enter a state park and that chains were required for all four tires. I was in my small Red Plymouth Duster filled with my clothes, my guitars and amps, my futon bed in the back seat, but no chains for my car. I continued on anyway, not wanting to turn back. Don't you hate backtracking and admitting to yourself you made a mistake?

I was amazed how steep the hill was that took me into the state park. It seemed like I was driving upward forever. The incline was so steep that my car tilted up like a rocket ship with gravity pulling my head back onto the headrest.

The asphalt turned into a dirt road only wide enough for one car. Eventually I saw a sign that showed I had just reached 7,000 feet above sea level, and it started to snow. Wow, what an adventure!

The pretty, gently falling snow turned into a full-out blizzard as the road wound around the steep mountain pass. I started to get nervous because I felt like I was getting in over my head. This was dangerous driving. Every once in awhile there'd be a break in the blizzard for a few seconds when the mountain shielded me from the wind, then I could see out my window. I was so high up I couldn't even see the bottom. I tried to stay cool, but there were no signs as to how much farther I'd have to drive like this. I hoped it wouldn't be too much farther.

Calmly, I asked God for help and protection. Eventually these requests turned desperate. My hands gripped the steering wheel so tight that my knuckles whitened and felt like they were welded onto the wheel. I started to have a hard time breathing. I thought at the time it was my anxiety, but it could have been the altitude.

I drove on like this for two and a half hours, mentally going into a zone of deep concentration and surrender.

Finally, the snow lightened up and the road began to slowly descend. Thank God! When it changed to blacktop, I said a blessing. After about another thirty miles I came upon another gas station and pulled in to find out how far I was from Flagstaff.

The woman said, "It's about twenty minutes down at the bottom of the hill, but the road is closed."

I asked her why and she replied, "A milk truck had been trying to make its delivery during the snow storm, jackknifed, hit the mountain, and now it blocked off any traffic going up or down the road."

"What are you trying to say?" I asked.

She said, "You can't get through."

"What are you telling me?" I tensed up.

She said, "You have to go back the way you came."

I gave her the most dead serious look I have ever given anyone and said, "There is no way I am going back that way," pointing up to the mountain.

She went back inside the gas station to check with one of the mechanics about an alternate route. When she returned, she told me that there was a little road off to the left that would take me back to the interstate highway.

"Is it a dirt road or blacktop?" I asked.

"Blacktop," she said.

I thanked her, and when I got back into the car, I thanked God for the blacktop road. Driving the forty-five minutes toward the highway, I really felt like a jerk. I had put my life in danger so unnecessarily.

After all the praying (actually begging for help would be more like it...) I was centered again and thanked God for protecting me. I was really sorry and humbled. I learned another valuable lesson about how important it is to listen to the Divine Inner Guidance.

When I reached the highway, the sign said I was getting back on at Exit 89. My four and a half hour detour over the mountain had only taken me one exit down from where I originally got off! OMG!

Hungry and disgusted, I drove down the highway wondering where I should get something to eat. I paid close attention to every ounce of inner guidance I received now.

I asked inwardly, "Should I get off here?"

The Inner Guidance said, "No."

At the next exit I asked again, "Is this my exit?"

"No, this one is not for you."

At the next exit five miles further, I asked for the third time, "Is this my exit?"

The Voice said, "Yes, this one is for you."

At the bottom of the hill was a big sign that read, "The Jackass Café."

9

Inner Music

*I*n 1985 while attending a spiritual seminar in Miami, I was asked to accompany a guitarist onstage. I hadn't started recording spiritual music yet. I had been playing recorder on and off since I was a kid. It's funny, even if I went a long time without playing the recorder, it always felt like I'd never stopped.

José, the guitarist, didn't want to play by himself and asked if I'd be willing to play the recorder along with him. I agreed and told him it wasn't necessary to send me a tape. I could just play along by ear.

Playing by ear is more like playing from the heart. Sometimes the spontaneity is inspiring, taking you places musically that you wouldn't normally go because you're in the moment. The word inspiration means "being in the Spirit in the moment."

Musicians can inspire each other like two artists with different brushes, painting on the same canvas. When you play along with another musician, you find your place in the painting—one instrument supports while the other takes the lead.

My friend Jeff Victor, a great pianist and producer, taught me that music and art are very similar. Each has a main subject, a background color or subject that creates a mood, and a setting. In musical terms, the chordal structure of the piano or guitar creates support for the lead instrument. The movement in the rhythm section of drums and bass drive the tempo and pulse of a song dictating the energy.

I arrived with my recorder at José's two-bedroom apartment. I was only playing one recorder at a time then. There were two adjacent bedrooms sharing a common wall and we were in the room on the left, just past the kitchen and bathroom. As he strummed some pretty chords I played along, improvising, and it sounded nice.

Since the door to his bedroom was open, when his sister entered the house I could see her walk past the kitchen and go into her bedroom, next to where we played. Apparently, she played the flute, because as I played, I could hear her harmonizing with me perfectly.

Then I started thinking, *How does she know what harmony to play? I'm improvising. How does she know what I'm going to play next when I'm just making it up as I go?*

This didn't make sense. I started to play unique

intervals and different rhythms that a traditional musician wouldn't normally play. And still she harmonized perfectly with me from the other room. I was baffled, but I was also really enjoying this jam session.

About fifteen minutes later, I stopped playing and said to José, "Wow, your sister is amazing on the flute! Why didn't you tell me she was such a great musician?"

"What do you mean?" José responded, "My sister doesn't play an instrument."

10

Two Flutes and a Puffy Shirt

*S*oon after arriving in Los Angeles, I got a jay-walking ticket for not crossing the street at the light. The ticket was $10 and I put it in my junk drawer. The very next day, about twenty miles away in a different part of Hollywood, I got a second jay-walking ticket. I also put that in my junk drawer. It felt like Candid Camera people were following me around dressed as policemen. After growing up in New York where no one crossed at the light, I thought it was rather bizarre to get these tickets two days in a row. My driver's license was from out-of-state, so I really didn't think I would have to pay them.

I was driving my little red Plymouth Duster through Beverly Hills practicing my creative visualization, imagining I was driving a red Porsche, and a third policeman pulled me over for going way above the speed limit. I put that ticket in my junk drawer with the other two.

Somehow they got my new address in North Hollywood and each month I was sent an updated ticket that doubled or tripled. After six months, each of my $10 jay-walking tickets had become $250 and my $80 speeding ticket grew to $400. They multiplied like bunnies. Warrants started coming in the mail for my arrest.

I'd never been to jail and wasn't aware of how serious these warrants were until Lou, my bass player, came over for lunch one day and saw the three warrants sitting on my counter. Apparently, Lou was familiar with these, so he explained to me, "If you're caught driving with just one of them, you will be put in jail immediately. And they'll take away your car. You cannot survive in Los Angeles without a car, so my advice to you is to pay a visit to each city hall and pay off the tickets right away."

I had $1,000 left in my bank account. The next day I drove all around the city to pay the $900 worth of tickets. This left me with only $100. I had to move out of my apartment the next day. I was at the end of my rope—thirty years old and my parents were finished bailing me out. (Years later, after I became successful, I contacted the woman who rented me the apartment and paid her back the two months of back rent to settle my karma. Her name was Tonya Williams, an actress from the soap opera, *The Young and the Restless*).

Anyway, now I was in real trouble. Thank God my

friend Lisa Solana allowed me to sleep on her couch for a short time while I figured things out. Lisa was a clothing designer who came up with half of the catalogue for a new company called Victoria's Secret.

I had been singing and playing acoustic guitar at some singer/songwriter clubs with a violinist named Mary Barton. Her friend Lisa had come down to watch us a few times and once said to me, "I've been playing my harp at Venice Beach on the weekends and making $200 a day." This sounded like a fortune to me—I was so broke.

I decided to go down to the beach myself the following weekend with one flute, a boom box with a tape of love songs, a tiny battery-powered Marshall amp, a basket, and a rose. I played for two hours and barely made a dollar. I gave the change I made to a homeless guy as I walked back up the boardwalk toward my car, a beaten man.

On my way, I also came across Lisa playing the harp accompanied by a guy with a weird sort of homemade harp-guitar.

"How'd you do?" she asked.

"Nothing," I said, and I told her what had happened.

I'm sure I looked terrible, because she said, "You're welcome to play with us for awhile. Maybe you can at least make your parking money back." Parking was

$6, and when you're down to your last $100, every dollar counts.

I started putting my flutes together when a woman on roller blades wearing a thong bikini whizzed by. Lisa's partner put down his guitar and ran down the beach after her.

Now Lisa didn't have anyone to play with, so she quickly prompted me to play along with her. There was no chair for me to sit on, so I sat down on the concrete of the boardwalk. *How can I get any lower?* I asked myself.

Since Lisa had only been playing the harp for three years, and since it's a very difficult instrument to play, especially with the sun shining in her eyes making it impossibly hard to see the strings, let's just say that she wasn't a virtuoso yet. I closed my eyes as we played, wondering, *Where is my life going?* and *How am I ever going to get out of this mess I'm in?*

When I opened my eyes at the end of the improvised song we'd just played, there was a crowd of people around us throwing money into her basket. From where I sat it looked like it was raining money. Then, I don't know why, but her partner soon moved back up to northern California.

The following week, Lisa and I made a tape with my last $100 at the cheapest recording studio in Los Angeles. A guy named Vince had advertised in the local musicians' magazine. We followed up on his ad and booked an evening to record. The studio was in his garage and he only charged $15 an hour. That's why we chose it.

It took us two hours to set up and two hours to record enough improvised music (with the six chords that Lisa knew) to fill the album. Each song was six or seven minutes long. I mixed the whole thing in two more hours. For the rest of my life I'll remember that 6 x $15 = $90. With the $10 I had left, we bought a pizza. We titled our tape *Celestial Winds*.

We found a pencil-drawn picture of a girl playing a harp and a guy playing a flute that we used for the cover. Lisa's roommate, who worked at the local Kinko's, made the copies for us. We'd made fifty copies of cassette tapes and colored the covers in with the magic markers and colored pencils that were free to use at the Kinko's counter. We figured that the other bands at Venice only had black and white tape covers, so adding the color would make us look more professional.

We didn't actually have the money to pay for the tape duplication, so I asked my friend Geno, who owned Straight Copy, if I could pay for them after the weekend. I had given him a fair amount of business previously, spending much of my money making copies of the rock music I'd recorded in Los Angeles.

The following weekend, we drove to the beach together in her car. As she drove I asked, "Does your gas gauge work? From where I'm sitting it looks like it's on empty."

"Yes," she said. "It's working." We had just enough gas to get to the beach.

That first day we sold almost all fifty cassette tapes. Then with each passing week we'd order more and sell them. I made just enough money to pay for a shared house with my friend Scott Lipps and another guy. (Scott later started a modeling agency called One-Management that became one of the biggest modeling agencies in New York.)

Something that really bugged me, though, was how much attention Lisa got from playing her Celtic harp and wearing her white linen dresses. She looked like a goddess with her long, dark, wavy hair blowing in the breeze. People would walk by and say, "Oh look at that beautiful woman with the beautiful harp." I was like the invisible man sitting there next to her.

Since she only knew six songs in the beginning, we had to play them over and over all day long. This is called torture for a musician. By late afternoon, we had played each of those songs about thirty times. I'd been bored out of my mind. Just to break up the monotony, every once in awhile I'd pick up a second flute and try playing two of them at one time in harmony. Whenever I did this, anyone walking by would say to their friends, "Hey look, there's a guy playing two flutes at once," and then Lisa became invisible! That was the only reason why I did it. It's funny that it became my trademark.

Another thing. Every time I played two flutes at one time, something else would miraculously happen—people would reach into their pockets to pull out money to buy a tape. Over the two years we played at Venice Beach, we sold more than 10,000 of these handmade, hand-colored tapes. Each one of them a real work of art.

I always wore a white Renaissance puffy shirt that Lisa found at a Salvation Army store. The writers of *Seinfeld* often came down to the beach on the weekends to relax and listen to us. Eventually this would inspire the famous episode of "The Puffy Shirt."

Never in my wildest dreams did I think that Venice Beach would turn into anything of value to me or my career. It was simply a way for me to make enough money using my musical talent to survive until the next week. It was also the first time I made any consistent amount of money from music since the AC/DC tribute band ten years earlier.

Venice Beach was the last place on earth I ever wanted to be, yet it was the most important thing I ever did. Without that experience of putting my ego aside and learning how to make a living using my creativity, I never would have had a career in music and you would not be reading this book. Divine Inner Guidance led me there, really looking out for my future and my best interest—-as always.

To view an excerpt from David's video *From Venice Beach to Woodstock,* enter **http:// www.DavidYoungMusic.com/video/Venice-Beach- to-Woodstock.wmv** in your browser.

11

Our Uniqueness Is Our Gift

When we look for direction in making a big decision, sometimes we have to be willing to venture outside our immediate sphere of familiarity. Our Divine Inner Guidance can see far into the future and far outside our immediate surroundings. In figuring out what to do with our lives and careers, we usually need all the help we can get.

My good friend Bobby Schnitzer, for many years my co-producer in Minneapolis, shared a story with me about Bob Dylan. Dylan grew up in Hibbing, Minnesota, a rural mining town about two and a half hours north of the Twin Cities. He moved down to St. Paul in the early 1960s to go to high school, and was in the same class as Bobby's older sister Loni. Dylan liked Loni's best friend and used to visit the Schnitzer house quite often.

Their basement had a piano and was the place where school friends would come over to get together.

Dylan didn't play the popular songs of the day. As a result of this fact and because of his unique sound when he played, all too often it would end the party. He was an avid songwriter, but the world had yet discover its appreciation for him.

Dylan booked a gig playing for free at a local pizza shop on a Saturday night, and Bobby, Loni, and their dad went to support him. Mr. Schnitzer was a businessman who felt bad for Dylan because he could see the love he had for music and that he was not being appreciated. Dylan was pretty much ignored during the performance. Afterward he sat down with the family and asked Mr. Schintzer for advice.

As kindly as he could, Mr. Schintzer said, "You need to go either to New York City or to Los Angeles where people are more open-minded and can appreciate what you have to offer."

The rest is history.

I think this story has never been recorded because the only people who heard that conversation were Bobby and Loni.

Bob Dylan ended up influencing more than a generation of songwriters, including John Lennon and George Harrison, who idolized him. His passion for writing songs with deeper meaning turned the Beatles from a pop group churning out love songs to music of social conscience with a powerful message. His lyrics are as inspiring and mind-opening as Jimi Hendrix's guitar playing.

I once met Artie Mogul, the man who signed Bob Dylan to his first international recording contract in New York. That was Dylan's big break—it made him a star. Mogul also signed Elton John and Peter, Paul and Mary, among many others.

When I asked Artie why he signed Dylan, he said, "Back in the day, artists would bring guitars into our offices to sing a few songs and audition. Dylan also had this bizarre metal contraption that I had never seen before that was hung around his neck with a harmonica attached to it. Between his odd voice and that contraption, I had to sign him. I'd never met anyone that unique." (Actually Artie didn't use the word 'unique,' but out of respect for Mr. Dylan I paraphrased it.)

It only takes a second to recognize Bob Dylan.

Our uniqueness is our gift. But we first have to accept it, then learn to appreciate it, and then accentuate and promote it. The very things that we usually don't like about our voice, our personality or what could be considered the weaknesses or blemishes of our art, often become the one thing that separates us from everyone else.

Robert Plant, the lead singer of Led Zeppelin, once said during an interview, "Whenever any song from the first four Led Zeppelin albums came on the radio, I immediately changed the station."

"How come?" asked the interviewer.

"I just can't stand the sound of my voice on those albums," he replied.

Every single musician I know would attest to the fact that the first four Led Zeppelin albums have the greatest, most unique, rock 'n roll singing ever recorded. Period. He changed the sound of rock singing forever.

Are Picasso, Dali, and Van Gogh remembered because of their technique or because they are still instantly recognizable? Their uniqueness is their fingerprint, their stamp. So is ours.

Our uniqueness is our gift.

12

Whoever, Whatever

My life had gone from having a beautiful wife and being a lead guitarist in one of the most popular touring bands in the Northeast, to a relationship lost and having nothing. So, there I was, now living alone in the basement of a Londonderry, New Hampshire farmhouse making $48 each weekend cleaning up the local Burger King. I didn't realize it at the time, but I had created this life for myself.

Eric Plummer, a fellow employee and new friend, arranged for me to live in his mom's unfinished basement in the country. Rent was $35 a week, which did include a peanut butter and jelly sandwich for breakfast, and there was an apple orchard with an unlimited supply of apples nearby. I was left with only $12 a week for myself.

Obviously I was depressed. No band, no girlfriend, no money, and nothing to do with myself from Monday to Friday, left me with no idea how I'd live through each day. It was almost impossible to get out of bed.

After a few weeks of this deep sadness, I realized that something had kept me alive through this horrible time—"WHOEVER, WHATEVER." I didn't know who God was or what It was, and I didn't want to exclude any of the possibilities, so that's why I called It: "WHOEVER, WHATEVER."

I greeted each day with, "Good morning Whoever, Whatever you are." Each night I'd say, "Thank you for getting me through another day Whoever, Whatever you are." The more I thought about the possibility that something actually cared about me, loved me and wanted me to succeed, the more I could feel Its presence. This lifted my Spirit as I started feeling connected to something greater than myself.

This was the beginning of my spiritual life.

13

Jonathan Livingston Seagull Leads
Me to the Flute of God

After about six months of being a weekend janitor, I had worked off my karma and decided to move back to upstate New York. I had some friends in the Cortland area who were involved in music and introduced me to a drummer who also wanted to start a project. Michael seemed like a nice guy and a decent drummer who lived about 90 minutes west of Cortland. I started spending so much time there that I eventually moved into his house so I wouldn't have to travel back and forth.

Michael had an uncle named Mark who was a fun-loving guy. He would come over to visit and I would overhear him talking about having experiences with spiritual masters with incredible names like Fubbi Quantz, Rebazar Tarzs, and Peddar Zaskq. Just the sound of these beings intrigued me.

Michael had a parking ticket that needed to be

paid about a half hour away in Bath, NY. He asked if I wanted to take a ride. I wasn't really in the mood and said I'd "stay behind and read a book." That was a joke. I didn't read books. (I hadn't looked at one since college five years earlier.) I only read rock magazines like *Rolling Stone* and *Circus*.

I went to his bookcase to see what he had and was amazed to see *Jonathan Livingston Seagull* by Richard Bach. Back in high school, every class but mine read that book and I always wondered why I hadn't. I'd see kids walking by in the hallway carrying it, and since it was a smaller than normal size paperback, it was always on top. There was something about it that always intrigued me. Actually, the two things I remember most about high school were the girl I had a crush on, Vicky Mitrani, and that book. Without a doubt, I was going to read it while Michael was out for a few hours.

Jonathan Livingston Seagull is about a bird that didn't think like everyone else and went beyond his own self-made limitations to become a hero. I devoured the book. It lit me up like a torch.

By the time Michael got back, I was jumping out of my skin and shared my excitement. "For the first time," I said, "I read something spiritual that I agree with and can believe."

"If you're that excited," he said, "Uncle Mark left

some books on Eckankar and Soul Travel. Maybe you'd like to take a look."

I decided that *The Flute of God* by Paul Twitchell would be the first book I'd read—especially considering the fact that the recorder was such a big part of my childhood—how could I not?

The book was deep. So deep that after about a month of only being able to digest one paragraph at a time, I asked Michael if there was another book that was easier to understand. *Eckankar, the Key to Secret Worlds* suited me better, and I've been studying the teachings ever since. The peace I have experienced in meditating with the word HU is beyond words. When people ask me about the spiritual feeling they get from my music, I tell them I find that peace from singing the HU.

Years later, the first book discussion class I taught was *The Flute of God*. Life is like an ongoing railroad that leads us to our ultimate place. When we learn all we need from one path, it's time to move on to the next track that will take us where we need to go.

Understanding Flying Dreams

Our producer in Toronto, Tom Treumeuth, recommended that I either sing or play guitar, since in the mid eighties that was the trend with rock bands. I decided to play guitar. He had received a tape from a singer named Livio in Springfield, Massachusetts, and we decided that I should go there to work with him for a few weeks to see what we could write together.

I remember the meeting that took place at Kevin D'Addario's house in Niagara Falls, New York. Tom called up Greyhound to find out how much a bus ticket from Buffalo to Springfield was. It was $48. I told him I didn't have any money. He reached into his wallet and took out a $50 bill and said, "This will get you there if you wanna go." That left me with $2 for myself once I got there. Livio's sister let me crash at her apartment and kindly fed me.

Livio was a talented singer, but from what I have experienced, it's typical for singers to be out of balance with their egos. (This is the only reason why I ended up singing later in life because it was impossible to deal with LSD, lead singers disease.) I lasted about two weeks working with him. That was all I could take.

I didn't know where to go since Buffalo had run its course and moving back to New York City was a painful thought. I decided to get a minimum wage job working for Hewlett Packard in Springfield, gluing some kind of new electronics together. It was a 12 hour shift that started at 6:00 a.m. The chips were used in these new things called computers. I had no idea what I was working on at the time, just that when the glue gun splattered and landed on my hands, it was really hot.

John Meyers, the light man from the AC/DC tribute band, was working with a band about an hour north of me. Northampton was a college town with a lot going on. One Friday after work I decided to hitchhike up to one of his gigs. As if by magic, I instantly got a ride that took me right to the club. John's band was doing pretty well and we chatted about old times in between sets.

While the band was playing, a middle-aged woman came to chat with me at the table where I was sitting alone. She said her niece had just broken up with her boyfriend and she was very beautiful. This woman definitely had quite a bit to drink, so I just listened and was cordial. Since she thought I looked so much like the guitarist of Motley Crue, her niece's favorite group, she wanted to fix me up with her and kept going on about this.

Finally I asked her if she had a picture of her. When she pulled out her photo I was surprised that she really was attractive. I told her to call her up and tell her I was in town for the weekend. She left a message that I was staying at John's house and gave his phone number. I forgot about it. (Obviously this was in the days before cell phones.)

Sunday morning at 10:00 a.m. the phone rang at John's. He said it was for me. I couldn't imagine who was calling me there. The woman on the phone said that her aunt had left her a message about me and she just received it. After a nice chat, she offered to take me out to lunch and I accepted.

John's house was out in the country, at least an hour away from where she lived in Northampton. After a quick shower I got back on the highway to start hitching. Everything seemed to be going as if it was carried by a beautiful breeze.

When I got to the side of the road, I put my thumb out as usual. After 10 minutes of standing there without getting picked up, my Divine Inner Guidance nudged me that I should go back in the house to ask John if I was heading in the right direction. Standing there for 10 minutes with no luck just didn't correspond with the good vibes of the day.

Of course, my Divine Inner Guidance was right on, as I was hitching in the wrong direction. Now on the right side of the road heading west, I got picked up by the second car that drove by. The man was going just a few blocks from where we were to meet at her aunt's house—about 70 miles away.

When I arrived, she was just as attractive as her picture and the attraction was mutual.

Her uncle was given the job of chauffeuring us around. Everything went just amazing. We had brunch, walked around, saw a movie, and then had dinner. I was planning on hitching back to Springfield at the end of the evening but her Uncle wouldn't allow that. He gave me the $12 for the bus back to Springfield. Before getting on, she said she'd like to get together again next weekend, but I couldn't. I was having a hernia operation the following Friday. I had also decided that I was going to be moving back to New York City, because I'd needed to recover from the surgery. So that was it. We hugged each other goodbye and said we would keep in touch by phone.

I worked the following week at my job and on Friday went into the hospital for my operation. After the local anesthesia kicked in, I was still half awake and could vaguely hear the nurses. By the sound of her accent, I could tell that one of them was Italian. My hair was very long. I was skinny and my arms were spread out wide on the operating table with the intravenous apparatus still attached. I heard her say to the other nurse, "He looks-a like-a Jesus!" That was the last thing I remembered.

When I came back to consciousness in the recovery room, I was groggy from the anesthesia, feeling very vulnerable. I was also sad that nothing was working in my life, plus I was alone in the hospital. After a half hour of sobbing, feeling sorry for myself, the nurse said that I had a visitor. I told her there must be some mistake since I really didn't know anyone around there. She left to check some things and came back to say there really was someone in the waiting room to see me. I said OK, not having a clue who it could have been.

The girl from Northampton had taken the bus down to make sure I was OK and wouldn't be alone. I was so touched by this that I started crying in front of her, covering my eyes. It felt like God was looking out for me and had sent her. She helped me leave the hospital and we got a cab that took me back to my apartment. I told her that nothing had worked out for me in Springfield and that I was going to head back to New York in a few weeks. If she wanted to visit me there I'd be happy to show her around. We said goodbye, and she left.

A few weeks later she came to the city to visit. I was

working at an entry level office job in Manhattan, so I at least had some money coming in. There are only two things I remember from that weekend.

The first thing is that since I was just back in New York, my friend Warren told me that the place to take her for a date was called "Windows of the World." This was a high-end restaurant at the top of the World Trade Center and should really impress her. Warren Bell came from a wealthy family that owned the biggest bagel bakery in New York, supplying bagels to most of the restaurants in the city. Unlike me, Warren had lots of money, and I had no idea how expensive that place was going to be. He and his girlfriend were going to double date with us. (Warren later became famous for inventing the 'bagel chip.')

The four of us met at the restaurant and had to wait about 45 minutes for a table even though we had a reservation. There was a little weird communication going on between the maitre'd and Warren that I was being kept separate from. Finally, Warren told me there was a problem. I was wearing a black velvet jacket with jeans (rock 'n roll style) and jeans were not allowed in the restaurant. That is why we hadn't been seated.

They were trying to figure out what to do with us. It was now 9:00 p.m. and we were all getting very hungry. We discovered that the only way for me to be allowed into the restaurant to eat would be to borrow an extra pair of khaki pants from a waiter. Humiliating as this was, I had to go along with it. From that point on, the evening was a downer for me.

After dinner we went back to the hotel, slept in separate beds, and I woke up the next day in a grumpy mood. It was obvious why I wasn't happy after the embarrassing incident at the restaurant, but I didn't understand why she had the blues. She didn't want to talk about it.

During breakfast she did open up. She seemed very self-conscious and said she didn't want me to judge her or think she was weird. Ever since she was a kid, she had unique dreams where she was outside her body, looking down at herself and sometimes flying away. It was always a nice experience but she was never clear about what was happening. Her parents took her to a few psychologists when she was younger, but none knew what this was. They also took her to a priest who did a special ceremony to make these experiences stop—but they continued.

The previous night with me in the next bed in the hotel room, she had another dream. It left her feeling sad that after all of those years, she still didn't understand them. When she woke up, she felt like something was wrong with her.

I asked her how she felt during the experiences. She said that while it was happening, it was beautiful. She was always happy. It was only after she woke up in the morning that she would think about it too much and turn it into a negative experience that no one could explain.

I told her that each of us has a Soul, and as we start to become more spiritual, our Soul wants to share with our conscious mind what amazing beings we really are. I had experienced that same thing of being in my Higher Self, separated from my physical body and feeling that freedom and happiness. I also shared that I had had many dreams where I was flying and it was the most exhilarating, incredible thing. Far beyond words.

I told her, "Just embrace and enjoy these experiences and know that God is giving them to you because He's showing you more of your True Self." She smiled and was visibly relieved. We finished breakfast, I took her to the train station, and we said goodbye.

I never saw her again. Her friendship and company was a gift to me when Spirit knew I needed a friend. Since I had followed my Divine Inner Guidance, I was able to receive the gift and also be a channel so she could understand herself better.

15

The White Van Appears

*I*n 1983 my brother Rob and I flew down to Florida to visit my dad. While swimming in the ocean in Miami, we became friends with Brad who was a mailman visiting from Toronto. He was about the nicest guy in the world, and from that moment on a magical friendship began that continues to this day.

A few years later, in 1986, I was living back in Brooklyn at my mom's house. I was lonely. It had been eight years since high school and I'd lost contact with most of my old friends. I decided to take the train into Manhattan to visit a drummer friend named Kevin, whom I hadn't seen since I was in upstate New York.

While I was walking to the station, I started an inner dialogue with "Whoever, Whatever." I had been meditating for about three years, so my inner connection with "It" had become an interactive part of my life. I had been reading something about how we can only receive as much as we can give and that gave me an idea. I told Whoever Whatever that if I had a woman in my life that I could love, then I would have more love to give to everyone I met. I also said I'd like her to have blond hair and an English accent. (You have to be specific, and the more specific, the better!)

When I got to the city, Kevin and I chatted for awhile at his studio and decided to get some lunch. He introduced me to his friend Bridget with blond hair from England—soon to become my second wife.

After dating for awhile, we decided to get an apartment together. On the day we were going to move her stuff in, some kind of miscommunication happened. All of her stuff was being put out on the street at the corner of 63rd and Madison Ave. She called me in a panic to do whatever I could. It was 5:00 p.m. and there were not many choices because our money was also limited at the time. I started calling old friends, but nothing was connecting. After two hours I'd exhausted every possibility and gave up. There was nothing I could do. I surrendered.

An hour later, my friend Brad from Toronto called. We would chat every three or four months just to stay in touch. He asked why I sounded so bummed out. I told him about Bridget's life-belongings being put out on the street in NYC and that I couldn't find a van to help her. It was now around eight o'clock, getting dark, and the inevitable was approaching.

Brad said that his friend Clarky's dad had a van and he could come get me. Then we could drive together into Manhattan to get her stuff to take it to our new apartment.

I said, "Brad, that's nice of you to offer, but you live in Toronto, nine hours away. By the time you get down to New York, it's going to be tomorrow morning. Then it'll be too late."

"Davey," Brad replied, "I just drove the van down from Toronto and arrived in Queens ten minutes ago. We unloaded a bunch of T-shirts from the van and it's empty now. I can be at your house in twenty minutes!"

This really happened. I was delirious. Everything worked out perfectly.

16

Loving What You Do

*W*hat can we do to get our kids to practice their instruments more?" I'm asked this question again and again by parents and interviewers.

As much as I'd love to hand them a magic answer, I have to be honest and tell them, "I have no idea. My parents did everything they could to get me to spend more time on my homework and practice my instrument less!"

When I think about it, though, it's all about inspiration. Inspiration is a unique animal. I've wondered, *Why do some people inspire us?* and *Why does some music touch us so deeply and profoundly?*

There are those who say our talents are gifts from God. I believe in God totally, but I've reached my own conclusion about this concept of the gift. If I hadn't practiced five or six hours every day when I was a kid, I would not have the abilities and talents I have now. This is what people call my gift.

So, in my observation, the true gift that God gives us is love. More particularly, we are born with a love for something. This love we have drives us and inspires us to practice, practice more, and eventually get better. It can be any discipline, craft, or purpose: art, music, cooking, gardening, the list goes on.

Bottom line ... the more we do this thing, the easier it becomes, and eventually it becomes effortless. Then, because we don't have to think about how to do it anymore, we can just put our heart, soul, and feeling into it.

Do you know why people call a performer great? A great performer looks like he's having the time of his life expressing his love for his music. His exhilarating experience shows in him while he's playing. We find joy in watching someone else blissing-out and sharing their gift with us.

This leads me to my story about Ray Charles.

I grew up in a white neighborhood in Brooklyn, New York in the 1960s, aware of the prejudice between colors of people. There were white kids and black kids in my school, but no black people were on our street or in our neighborhood. I always thought it was ironic that the tough Italian kids in my school, who were so prejudiced toward black kids, only listened to music made by black artists.

Every once in awhile, when I was watching TV, there would be a commercial for *Gospel Greats* which featured black singers singing with incredible feeling, power and emotion. I was touched by this music and wanted to buy these recordings. However, my dad didn't like the idea much, and it was not open for discussion.

I was allowed to buy Led Zeppelin, Bad Company, and other British rock albums sung by white artists, though. It was interesting because the more I would read about my favorite rock singers like Robert Plant, Paul Rodgers, and Steve Marriott, the more I saw that the singers who influenced them the most were black singers like Ray Charles, Aretha Franklin, Howlin' Wolf and Muddy Waters. Some of these great artists started out as gospel singers. So when I saw this pattern in so many of my idols, I realized that I could go to the same source that inspired them and find a clue to their greatness.

A few years later, around 1974, I was at the Kings Plaza Shopping Mall in Brooklyn and found my first Ray Charles album in the $2.99 rack. I figured that $2.99 was a worthwhile investment to find out what had inspired so many of my idols.

When I got home and started to listen, I was a little disappointed because there were no loud rock 'n roll guitars and drums. I could definitely hear why my heroes were inspired by Ray's voice. There was so much feeling in it! Ray was the real thing. He sounded like he was having so much fun. Other times his pain was so real you could feel it. As a listener, you had no choice but to believe every word and get carried away by it. As a musician, if you loved music, you had no choice but to be inspired by him.

Many years went by and, get this, I had the good fortune to run out of money. Playing my flutes at Venice Beach gave me a career playing peaceful instrumental music. It was absolutely the last thing in the world I ever thought I'd end up doing, in the absolute last place on this earth I ever wanted to be playing.

One thing led to another and eventually our little harp and flute duo, Celestial Winds, began to make a name for itself. People called us the Angels of Venice because we always wore white and the music was always so peaceful. They also used to say there was an energy around us like a "bubble of love." Tourists would stumble upon us and take our tapes home with them as great little pieces of memorabilia, but the locals would come down to meditate while we played, knowing we'd always be there on the weekends.

For the record, the reason why we always wore white was to separate us from all of the crazy people who were around. I used to say that Venice Beach was "the Noah's ark for the psychic and insane." We had to take special measures to make ourselves look approachable, safe to talk to, and safe to buy a tape from.

White was a sign of peace, of spirituality, that made us look trustworthy and different from all of the nut cases there. I guess white was also a sign of surrender for me. I had no choice but to be there playing the flutes every weekend. It was the only way I could make enough money to live on. I really would've preferred to be playing the guitar and rocking out.

The Los Angeles Times did an article on us when we'd sold our first 50,000 copies. Then CNN decided to do a three-minute feature story / interview that traveled around the world in many languages.

After the World Trade Center was bombed the first time in 1993, the event planner who was coordinating the gala reopening party saw us being interviewed on CNN.

He offered us a lot of money to fly to New York and open for Ray Charles, the headliner of this very special event. This was a chance for me to see Ray Charles up close. It meant a lot to me, as you can well guess. He is a musical legend. As I said, he inspired a host of artists from the 1950s through the 1970s in one way or another.

We got to the venue around 4:00 p.m. to do our sound check, but Ray was still on stage with his band running through songs in their repertoire. A sound check is a chance for the band to check their equipment and monitors to make sure everyone can hear themselves and each other. It's a technical process, not a performance. You know, check-one-two, check-one-two . . . Ray was rocking out, swinging his head around, his feet flying up in the air.

We just stood there transfixed on the dance floor, watching this personal performance. After two or three songs, Ray's manager, a very distinguished black man, walked up and stood next to me. He saw the look on my face as I stood watching Ray and appreciating this priceless opportunity.

After a moment, I asked him, "If this is just the sound check, then why is Ray jumping around like it's a real performance?"

"Because no one loves Ray's music as much as Ray," he replied.

When Ray's body moves, it's not because he's trying to impress anyone out in the audience. It's because the music is moving him.

People love watching great entertainers because they are having so much fun doing what they love.

I met six-time Grammy-winning saxophonist David Sanborn backstage at a concert in 2009 when my friend Ricky Peterson played keyboards with him. Sanborn was telling someone next to me that his inspiration for playing the saxophone was from listening to Ray Charles' sax player.

I related my story about being at Ray's sound check

and that "no one loved Ray's music as much as Ray." Though I didn't know Sanborn at all, that story gave me credibility.

Sanborn said, "There you have it. Nothing more need ever be said about music. That's why we do what we do."

To download David's unique and inspirational version of "America the Beautiful," either capture the QR code with your mobile device or enter **http://tinyurl.com/722gys6** in your browser.

17

The Miracle of Empty Boxes

*W*hile we were playing at the beach every weekend, I began to notice a pattern. Whenever a massage therapist or a spa owner came to our table, they would buy everything we had!

I thought about looking into advertising in a magazine specifically for spas, but my Divine Inner Guidance never gave me the go-ahead to buy an ad. A sales rep called me once a month for about six months, so I got to know her pretty well. She told me that the Los Angeles Spa Show was coming up and that I should think seriously about getting a booth. I never thought of that.

The rest is history. For seven years, I was the only booth with music in an industry that needed music all day long to create a spiritual mood for their clients. My area looked like feeding time at the zoo. Every day attendees bought hundreds of CDs, leaving piles of empty cardboard boxes. I started calling the space behind my booth "The Miracle of the Empty Boxes."

This also served a spiritual purpose for millions of people. During a facial or a massage, clients had their eyes closed and were encouraged to relax. This was an excellent opportunity for people to drift off or meditate and be touched by the spiritual energy in my music.

Today, if you get a massage or facial treatment practically anywhere in North America, there's roughly a 50/50 chance that you're listening to me.

18

HELP!!!

After four and a half years of living together and two and a half years of being married with a prenuptial agreement, Sophia and I decided to call it quits. This will sound bizarre, but since I was making great money for the first time in my life, the biggest problem we had was that I wanted to buy her things; clothes, etc. and she never felt comfortable with that. You wouldn't think that that would ever be a problem in a relationship! She was a super kind, gentle person, but I was nine years older and we didn't really connect in some other important ways. I felt like we had grown apart, becoming more friends than lovers. We had slept in separate bedrooms on and off the whole year.

After a bad experience at the International Spa Show in Las Vegas, we had "the talk." I told her that since I'd been divorced twice before, I wanted to make the transition as easy as possible for her and offered that she could live in my $500,000 Los Angeles house (that I bought with my own money) for as long as she wanted. Since I was traveling 40-45 weekends a year, I decided I would just spend time in other places. Sophia was my bookkeeper/office manager, and I had four full-time employees shipping CDs out to my 1,500 wholesale accounts all week long. I wanted her to keep working for me so she wouldn't have to look for another job. My business was doing incredibly well, bringing in between $350-$400,000 a year, and I was the success story of the independent music biz.

A few weeks later, I decided to fly up to Seattle to visit a friend named Faith, who was also a psychic.

When I opened my safe to get some money for the trip, I clearly heard God's voice inside telling me, "Take the money with you." So I took all the money I had in envelopes out of my safe and put it in my suitcase to keep at Faith's house. It felt warm and comforting knowing that I was being guided and that God was looking out for me. I could really feel God's love for me.

The taxi was already a half-hour late. I kept calling, getting angrier each time I called because I didn't want to miss my flight. Eventually I got really pissed off. I decided it was ridiculous for me to take all that money up to my friend's house in Seattle. I put the money back in the safe. God's voice spoke to me a second time, "Take the money with you." But that didn't make any sense. I trusted Sophia more than God's voice.

While I waited for the taxi, considering there was so much change going on in my life, I decided to do a technique with one of my Eckankar books. First I said a little prayer for guidance and tried to focus. Then I randomly opened up the book *Stranger by the River* by Paul Twitchell and read a paragraph to get a message from Spirit. This is what I opened to, "When the Voice of God comes to you, it is a gift. Obey or you will suffer the rest of your days."

I called the taxi again and got even more angry. It was 5:00 a.m. and I was now tired and grumpy. As I locked the safe with the money back in it, I actually said to myself, "God, I know you want me to take this money, but I'll find out why later." The taxi eventually showed up and I left.

When I arrived in Seattle, I told Faith that Sophia and I were finally ending our relationship, but that things were good between us. I said I wanted to help her in every way because we were friends and I cared about her. Faith said, "There's someone else involved." I didn't understand what she was talking about.

Faith had died in a car accident a few years earlier and when she reached the white light after the tunnel, the angels there said she had a choice, to stay in Heaven or to go back to earth. She said she wanted to go back to earth to help with the lifting of mankind, and instantly she was back in her body at the hospital.

Ever since then, she just knew things. A few days later, while at a park called Deception Falls, I spoke to her again about Sophia. She said, "There's someone else involved."

I returned to Los Angeles. Sophia was away on a trip to Miami to see about the possibility of an acting job there. I paid for her trip to help her.

On the morning when my assistant and good friend Jeff Ross (who used to sing in Badfinger) came to take me to the airport for a five-week road trip, I had an awful pain in my solar plexus. I'd been up most of the night.

Since Jeff worked with me and knew that I had money in my safe, he asked if his wife Diane should take it home with her, since Sophia and I were splitting up.

"It isn't necessary," I said. "We're ending as friends and I trust her completely. She never wanted anything from me financially anyway." (I actually trusted her more than I trusted God's voice. What a gigantic mistake!)

On August 1, 2000, the fifth day of a five-week road trip, I got a call from her attorney. Sophia was suing me for half of the business I started before I met her and half of my house that was worth $500,000 at the time. Since California is a community property state, she had the right to half of it. The prenuptial agreement did not hold up.

Sophia fired all my employees, closed my office and paid them extra to find other jobs and never come back. She canceled my credit cards so I couldn't fly back to see what was going on. Fortunately, I had frequent flyer miles on every airline, so I was able to get a flight back the following day.

My safe was emptied and $12,800 was stolen from it. Half of my furniture was gone and so was our dog Buddy, the little black and white Chihuahua on the front cover of the CD *Life Stories*. There was no one to answer the phones in the office, and I had to fly back later that same day to finish the five-week tour. I developed a heart condition. I kept traveling, trying to keep everything going, and stopping into hospitals along the way.

A mutual friend of ours found out what was going on and told me that Sophia had wanted to leave with her own stuff like we'd agreed to early in our relationship (my stuff was my stuff and her stuff was her stuff...) but her mom, who also worked for me, told her, "If you are not going to take half of David's money, then I am going to take it in your name." I married Sophia and basically got divorced from her mentally unstable mother! The money from the safe was used to pay their rent and food expenses for the next five months until the divorce was final. Without that money, they could not have taken anything from me without going to jail.

A few days later, I found out she also had half ownership rights to every song I wrote (and every CD I had made) while we were together. I checked into a mental institution in Minneapolis. I was only in there for a day. It scared the hell out of me. My friend Jeff convinced them to let me out by showing them my CDs and product catalogue, telling them that I was in town to perform.

We drove directly from the hospital to the Eckankar Temple located in Chanhassen, Minnesota, about thirty minutes away. I told one of my good friends who worked there what had just happened, and she suggested that if I wrote a letter to my spiritual teacher, Harold Klemp, she would give it to him. I wrote the letter and added that Sophia was now part owner of all of the spiritual music that I had donated to Eckankar which had become part of their seminars and CDs. I wasn't sure what was going to happen next.

Since I had just finished *Deep Spirit*, I signed a CD for my friend to give to him.

Dear Sri Harold,
    Help!!!
David Young

The next day, I performed at the Uptown Art Festival in Minneapolis, losing it inside myself, but still able to play my peaceful music. I sold $12,800 of CDs in three days. It was the exact amount that they'd stolen from my safe.

After that I had to fly to Seattle for the next show. Faith was unavailable, but had her sister Marilee who lived on one of those little islands across the water from the city meet me at a place called "Point No Point."

I took the ferry across in my rental car, then drove an hour into the middle of nowhere to a tiny little grocery store by the beach. I told Marilee what had happened and that it was great to see her and have someone to talk to. After awhile she said she had to go back to work and asked me what I was going to do next.

"I think I'm going to take a walk down this beach and just sit there for awhile," I said. I had no place to go the rest of the day.

We said goodbye and she drove off.

I walked all the way down the winding beach to a cove. There was a long dead tree washed up on the shore. I decided to sit down there and rest, just looking at the water. I wondered what was going to become of my life since I might lose everything I had worked my whole life to achieve. I'd traveled 45 weekends each year to build my business and now my business was closed down.

I reached out spiritually to the angels that I have

come to know as the ECK Masters. I surrendered and opened my heart as wide as I could and spoke to them, asking them for their help.

As I let go, a calmness came over me, and I felt closer to them than I ever had. They were all around me and I could feel their love and support. I realized that whatever happened, even if I lost everything, I still had the one thing that I started my career with: my flutes and my talent. If I had to rebuild the whole thing from nothing, then that's what I was going to do.

I continued to surrender, saying, "God, it's all in your hands."

And I felt better. I laughed a little, thinking about what a mess I was in. I smiled as I looked out over the water with Seattle off in the distance.

The angels gave me a nudge to look over my left shoulder and look down, so I did. Right next to where I was sitting, in a little fire pit in the sand, was a wooden log that had been part of a campfire. Written in charcoal letters in my handwriting—just as I had written on the CD to my spiritual teacher—were the letters HELP!!!

From the detached spiritual state I was in, I wasn't even surprised to see it. I knew that wherever I went, Divine Love was going to be with me, that I was never alone and I would always get the help I needed.

The following weekend I sold $12,800 at the next show.

The weekend after that I sold another $12,800.

I got the message. Spirit was going to give me everything back I had lost and more. But I gained an incredible lesson about how valuable it is to listen to Divine Inner Guidance.

19

God Has a Sense of Humor

*W*hile performing at the Atlanta Gift Show in 1999, I noticed a man in deep thought standing about twenty yards away from my booth. An inner nudge urged me to go over and talk with him on my next break.

"I love your music," he said, after I'd introduced myself to him. "I just wish I could think of a way that our companies could work together." I noticed the company letters N-B-S under his name on the badge he wore.

"Hmm, NBS," I remarked. "What does that stand for?"

"Oh, it stands for the National Bridal Society. We're the biggest bridal service in the world with over 5,000 consultants."

Another nudge, the wheels were turning in my head, and an idea came to me.

"I could make you a CD called the *Perfect Wedding* CD by taking the six traditional songs from my Merry Christmas album and adding another six love songs," I said. "It would only take me a few days to record the other songs."

We walked back to my booth and I played a little of "Pachelbel's Canon," "Amazing Grace," "Jesu," "Ode To Joy" and "Ave Maria" on the sound system.

"I love this idea!" he exclaimed. "Let's do it." We exchanged cards.

Next came the difficult part—getting our lawyers to agree on how to do this project legally. Three months and $3,000 later, I finally called N-B-S with an idea.

"These lawyers are getting nowhere and just wasting our money," I told him, then suggested, "This is how I think we can do this. I'll pay to record the six new songs and combine them with the other ones. I'll manufacture CDs for you with your logo and any artwork you design for your *Perfect Wedding* CD. You will own the rights to your packaging. I'll manufacture my CDs with my own artwork and call it *Sacred Love Songs*. You can just pay me for whatever you order with a minimum of 1,000 CDs."

"Let's do it."

We had the contract written up and I got started.

Perfect. Except for the fact that six months had

passed since our initial meeting and I now had to record the other songs for the *Perfect Wedding* CD in the middle of a horrendous divorce! I'd have to stop in the middle of a take in the studio to answer calls from my very expensive Los Angeles attorney!

Now here's where God shows a perfect sense of humor.

Sacred Love Songs became the biggest selling CD I have ever had. Up to that point, stores would order three to six copies of my CDs at a time, but *Sacred Love Songs* was ordered by the dozen. Some stores even ordered boxes of 100 each month! If there was ever a CD that was a hit in the gift market, that was it.

20

Bloomington Once a Month

*W*hen I finished recording the CD, *The Mystery of Destiny*, someone recommended that I hire Los Angeles photographer Zarek to shoot the cover. This was the instrumental CD, not the rock opera musical *Woodstock, the Mystery of Destiny*.

Zarek and I spoke on the phone and he seemed like a nice guy who knew what he was doing. We set up the shoot for the following week. Then out of the blue, he called me a few days later and said, "David, I just had a vision for your album cover."

My intent was really just to hire him to take a photograph, but I was polite and let him share his idea.

"I see you with one foot in black and white in a big city on one side," he said, "and your other foot is in color, heading into green hills in a country setting."

Divine Inner Guidance confirmed that this was a very good idea. I put my ego aside and, for the first time, I allowed someone else to creatively design one of my CD covers.

When I arrived at the studio to take the photo, he said, "I also arranged for my niece to come to the session, so it would appear that you're following a little girl from the city into the country."

I worked hard to stay open minded, but he was crossing the line by adding someone else to my CD cover. I resisted but agreed in the end to a few shots with the little girl, just to make him happy.

We blended seven different pictures together in Photoshop to create the background with the girl leading me from the city into the country. This did become the front cover of *The Mystery of Destiny*, and since then I've never had so many compliments on a cover!

The following year, as the dust was settling from the divorce with Sophia, Annaliise, my daughter from Bridget, started reaching out to me for the first time. She just turned thirteen and was entering a difficult period.

I contemplated what I could do to help her as I was on my way to the Philadelphia Spa Show. I decided to start spending one week each month with Annaliise in Minneapolis. The following day at the convention, a sales rep named Emma came to my booth to talk to me about distributing my music. She sold relaxation tanks and wanted to sell my CDs along with them.

When she handed me her business card, I saw that her office was in Bloomington, Minnesota. "You know, my daughter Annaliise lives in Bloomington. I just decided yesterday to visit her once a month in between shows."

"My two daughters and I live close to Bloomington," she said, "so next time you come to visit your daughter, we should all get together."

Three weeks later, I flew to Minneapolis and stayed there. Emma and I were together for nine years. Zarek's vision for my CD cover was prophetic. I moved from the big city of Los Angeles, to the peaceful green hills and calm of this nice Midwestern Minnesota town.

21

Where Is the Waterfall?

*I*n preparation for a talk on the spiritual purpose of music, I contemplated on the subject. My Divine Inner Guidance gave me this clue: God created the different instruments so people would eventually be able to talk about and describe the sound in each of the different heavenly worlds.

This made sense because there is a world that sounds like a thousand violins, a world that sounds like bagpipes, a world with the single note of a flute, plus many others. These sounds give us a clue to where we are when we are meditating or dreaming in the Inner Worlds.

Here is an example. I took a girlfriend to a group meditation where we sang the spiritual word HU together with about twenty-five people. This is the sound that I meditate with. It's also the source of the peace and spirituality in my music. Most people have heard of the word OM and have used it as a mantra along with their yoga practice. I've heard people say that OM grounds them with the earth while HU opens up the heavens.

After everyone sang HU for about twenty minutes, they sat in quiet contemplation. This is my favorite part because I can hear the sound of Spirit vibrating inside me.

The room was now very quiet, and Emma whispered something to me. It sounded like she said, "Where is the water fountain?"

"What?" I asked her. I wasn't sure I heard her right.

"Where is the water fountain?" she whispered again.

"It's down the hall by the bathroom on the way out," I replied. Soon after that we left the room and approached the bathroom in the hallway.

"I don't see it," she said.

"See what?" I asked.

"The waterfall. Where is the waterfall?" she asked.

"There's no waterfall here," I said.

"I heard a waterfall in the room while we were chanting HU. You said it was out here by the bathroom?" she said.

"I thought you were looking for a water fountain.

There is no waterfall in this building," I replied.

Emma thought I was playing games with her.

"Can we go back to the meditation room to see if there was a waterfall?" So we headed back there, but by this time someone had locked the door and the area was closed off. The director said we'd have to come back another day. This increased Emma's curiosity because she still wasn't sure whether I was playing a joke on her.

We returned a few days later and took part in a short tour of the temple building that housed the meditation room we'd been in before. When we walked into that room again during the tour, the guide asked if we'd like to do a short HU. Everyone agreed, so for the next few minutes we all closed our eyes and sang. A beautiful peace filled the room.

"Did anyone experience anything?" the tour guide asked.

Emma stood up and told her story. "I was here a few days ago and while I sang HU, I heard the sound of a waterfall. Then afterwards, when we were outside by the restrooms, I didn't believe it when David told me there was no waterfall in here. So we came back today for me to prove to myself what I heard.

"When we arrived and entered this room it was silent, but once we started singing HU, the sound of the waterfall came back to my inner ears again."

This proved to Emma that she definitely heard the Inner Sound.

22

Creativity:
The Worst that Became the Best

*E*ach CD I record has its own unique story. Some of my early albums took months of "pre-producing" the songs in my head. Later on, because I was so busy, some just "came out of me."

Music is like painting. If you write a melody or a song before recording it, you have a sound in mind. In art that would be called "realism" because you are trying to replicate something already existing in your mind or your vision. If you don't have an image in mind and you're just creating in the moment, you're "improvising." In art, it's often "abstract" or "surreal."

Sometimes it's easier to improvise, other times, not. I can say that after recording over 50 albums of music, when I listen back to each of them, the songs I enjoy the most now are the ones that were the most difficult to make sound great. For a parent, it's like the kid who gave you the most trouble ending up being something special and winning a deeper love than you could have thought possible. These were often songs I'd be so unhappy with during the recording process that I'd want to give up on them. But I kept making attempts to find something that would save it.

My favorite example of this is the song "Divine Transformation" on my *Solace* CD. My co-producer, Bobby Schnitzer, and I now call it "the worst-song-that became-the-best song."

Solace was unique because I knew I had to record an album for a Las Vegas Spa Show at the time. I always had to have a new CD for it. It was the biggest spa event each year, my number one show for selling music to massage therapists and estheticians. One year I actually sold 2,800 CDs in 3 days. I had two people helping me sell the CDs at the table, and one other person emptying the boxes and restocking the table. The three of us couldn't reload the table fast enough. OMG, those were the days!

At the time I was writing the musical *The Mystery of Destiny*, making the film *Village of Dreams*, developing a series of musical cards, plus traveling 40 weekends that year. I arrived at the studio without one song, one chord, or even one note prepared.

"What are we going to start with?" Bobby asked when I arrived.

"I have no idea," I said. Actually, I also said, "Why are you asking me?" That had become our joke when

I knew I was going to have to fake my way through an album and start improvising.

We'd recorded fifteen albums of music together by then, about four albums a year, so Bobby was used to working with me on musical adventures. But I'd never started a project with less direction than this. I had nothing. A totally blank canvas. Not one idea.

Somewhere between the front door, saying hello, and walking over to the console in the studio, I had a flash. It was Divine Inner Guidance. I suddenly remembered a jam session Robin Berry and I had recorded a few years earlier. We'd never used it.

Robin was the harpist who played on *Ancient Treasures, Creation, Candlelight I* and *II,* and *A Christmas Dream.* Bobby couldn't remember the session, but I did. I just couldn't recall what year it was. There were nine different reels of music that I'd recorded there. Finding this one was going to take awhile.

Luckily, the first reel he opened from four years earlier was the one! Lucky guess? Divine Inner Guidance? It could have taken a whole day. There were about 200 untitled songs to go through.

Robin had just recorded a new album in 2003, and Bobby had just found a new way to position the microphones in the room. It was the best sound he'd ever gotten with her harp, so he called me, saying, "You need to come over and record something with Robin!"

I'd just written a nice guitar chord progression that morning. We recorded it along with about five improvisational sessions on the spot.

These recordings became the foundation of the *Solace* CD. My challenge was to take these old jams and turn them into gems. It's like shooting a bunch of pictures then attempting to turn them into a movie with a beginning, a middle, and an ending. Some sections we'd improvised were good but only happened once. I decided to repeat these sections and add something different to them each time. This changed them from just a "free form" abstract improvisation into more of a song.

Bobby didn't agree with my approach, though. He is a super musician, producer, and guitarist. He played in the band Lips Inc., which made the song "Funkytown," one of the most played songs ever. He thought the jams should just stay jams. He kept saying, "Don't try to make this into a song." But an inner voice kept directing me to do what I was doing. I really can't say I produced this album because I had no idea where it was going. But I was on a mission to get it there.

Since there were no words attached to these pieces, we had to give each song a working title so each computer file would have a name. Some of these were goofy titles like "Skulls" because we'd used an ethnic percussion sound called skulls on one song. I knew that title wasn't going to stick. You can't have a song called "Skulls" on a relaxing New Age album.

Another song we'd dubbed "The Call of the Wild." I don't remember why I called it this, but the title sounded too much like a 70s classic rock song. Since all of the music sounded like a journey taking you somewhere, the working title of the album was *Sojourn*. I couldn't think of a name for one of the songs, so I just called it "Sojourn," figuring it would be the title track. We kept changing the titles during the process. I'm telling you all this to show how it was a constant creative process of making things up, perfecting, improvising, and surrendering to Divine Inner Guidance.

Things began to take shape, but there were not enough songs for a complete album. I had just recorded some electric twelve-string guitar on one of the songs when Bobby got a serious health-related phone call and we had to take a break. My intuition told me to play something peaceful since Bobby was so stressed out on the phone. I experimented with something that sounded very East Indian and had the idea to retune the guitar like a sitar. Then one of the twelve strings broke, so now there were only eleven strings on the guitar.

By the time Bobby got off the phone, I'd finished writing the song. "Mind if we stop what we're doing so I can record this new thing I just wrote?" Bobby eventually got used to working with me. It's been a process for him, too—LOL. This song was "the worst-song-that-became-the-best song," "Divine Transformation."

The problem was that the guitar was made for hard rock music. It was the same kind of double neck guitar that Jimmy Page used in Led Zeppelin. I played it with a clean sound instead of a distorted rock sound, but it never sounded ethereal enough. It sounded too much like what it really was—out of place on this album.

All the other songs had harp and recorder. Some had a touch of acoustic guitar and had a style or a sound to it. Robin was unable to come in to play the harp on this, for one reason or another, so I just kept adding everything I could on top of it to make it fit in with the rest of the songs. Each song needed to be beautiful, relaxing, and ethereal. Oh my God did this song drive me crazy. It was trying to fit a square peg into a round hole.

I'd learned from producing so many albums that continuity is ultimately important in the success of a CD. I had sold music to over 10,000 massage therapists and spas and the one comment/compliment I'd consistently heard was that there were no surprise songs that ruined the vibe of an album, like so many of the other CDs they'd try to sell. This song did not fit in with the rest of the musical pictures. It would ruin the continuity.

Time was running out. We started the final mix-
ing process of all the songs. We'd work on this song,
then give up and finish something else. After everything was done except this song, we worked with
it for two more days. Each of the other songs took
only two hours to mix. I took it home, listened to it,
and hated it. I decided it was not going to be on the
album. No song had ever frustrated me that badly.
The main instrument, the electric guitar, just didn't
sound spiritual enough. Just thinking about this song
brings back the uptight, frustrated feelings I had from
the experience.

The next morning I woke up, listened to it, still
hated it, and surrendered. Then an idea came to me:
How I could literally double the special effects on the
guitar—the reverbs, delays, and harmonizing effects
to make it more ethereal. We tried every gadget and
available sound in the studio on top of it! Bobby found
an extra unit and picked the perfect effect. It finally
became something else.

Since the song was such a process that took on a life
of its own and was transformed, I changed the name
to "Divine Transformation." Whenever I played this
song at a show, once the album was finished, it pro-
jected so much vibe and spiritual energy that people
were mesmerized and drawn to my table like nothing
I had ever seen before.

Now comes the best part of the story.

I decided to change the title of the album to *Solace*. "Skulls" became "Divine Transformation." "The Call of the Wild" became "Calling All Souls." Almost every song had gone through one or two title changes except the song "Solace." I also changed the order of the songs at the last minute.

When I listed them all together on the back of the CD, I could see, with the final order of the titles in place, they became a sentence. The Ancient Dialogues are Calling All Souls on a Sojourn to The Zen Master who brings Solace and Divine Transformation of Heaven and Earth—Ascendance. A sentence!

I had trusted my Divine Inner Guidance and something incredible was created from a bunch of random pieces that were going nowhere and were not connected. Even the title now had meaning and magic to it.

And the happy ending to the story? *Solace* was nominated for a Grammy that year for Best Instrumental Album.

The following year I decided to put a rock group together called Namasté. I wrote words for "Calling All Souls" which became "Forever One" and did the same with "Divine Transformation" which became "Until I Found You." If you go to **DavidYoungRocknSoul.com** you will be able to watch the two music videos made for these songs.

23

The Three Golden Keys

*I*t seems like so many of my stories have an element of conflict in them. Overcoming obstacles is a form of conflict. The strange thing is that in our personal lives, we do everything possible to avoid conflict, but the movies we enjoy most have the most conflict. This is what we call entertainment, watching other people in conflict.

When I started writing my first movie, Sim Sarna, a Los Angeles friend of mine asked me, "What do you know about screenwriting?"

"Over the years," I told him, "many incredible things happened during my travels, and when I came home, my friends loved to hear me tell these stories. They said I was a good storyteller."

Sim had been a film major at UCLA. His mom and dad ran a company in the gift business and designed gifts that were sold everywhere in the United States. They always played my music in their showroom in Atlanta, and that's where our friendship began.

Sim was able to get funding to produce his first film soon after he graduated. It was a low-budget comedy called *College Vacation*. Incidentally, a low budget film costs less than five million dollars to make. He hired a few of his friends in Los Angeles who were unknown actors.

Sim's good luck came the following year when three of these actors, including Bradley Cooper, were cast in the biggest comedy of the year, *American Pie*. All of a sudden, because of the demand for these actors, Sim's movie became a hit. Blockbuster ordered thousands of them, EMI picked up the distribution rights, and he had a career in the film industry.

After studying filmmaking for years, Sim wanted to help me make the best film I could. During a lunch break at the gift show, he asked me these questions:

"What are the three parts of a story?"

"Hmmm, let me think about this for a minute." I didn't know, but I didn't want to look stupid. "The beginning, the middle, and the end?"

"Right!" he said. I don't know who was more surprised, him or me.

Then he asked, "What is the most important element in a story? Every film has it. Without it, a film stinks."

After thinking about it, I admitted, "I don't know."

"Conflict," he said. "Every character has to overcome a conflict that he rises above. Otherwise, the audience feels like nothing important has happened. Without conflict, a movie or a story is called boring or lame."

He continued, "What is the conflict in your movie, *Village of Dreams*?"

"Harald Wohlfahrt and I just want to make a movie of Christmas music in the medieval Bavarian village of Rothenberg and beautiful surrounding countryside in Germany. We want a sense of peace, not conflict."

"You have to have a conflict or it will be a terrible movie," he countered.

Up to that point, everything had been going swimmingly as we filmed. Magical things happened every day. We started filming in January and if we needed snow, it would snow that day. If we needed clear skies, the weather would be beautiful.

I originally had the idea to make the *Village of Dreams* movie while performing under the giant white indoor Christmas tree in Katie Wohlfahrt's Rothenberg store. I'd been playing there for twenty days and it had been very successful. I thought, This would be the best place in the world to make a music video. One idea led to another, and it grew into the making of the film. I had hoped this would be good publicity for my career and take me to the next level where I could do more concert performances. It was also something

Harald could sell in his stores, and I could sell to all of my wholesale accounts in America.

Our original budget was 20,000 Euros. We each agreed to pay half. We hired the best film crew in Munich, which was two hours away. He had 250 employees there that were able to help. We didn't need to do any set construction. Harald owned half the town of Rothenburg, and the main scenes were shot inside his 10,000 square foot store. If there could be a North Pole on earth, this was it! The German Christmas museum, another of his properties, was also right next to the store. It's the most well known museum of its kind.

I met Harald at the Atlanta Gift Show. He came upon my booth on his way out of the show after going through the whole thing and not making one purchase. Back in those days my booth was always busy with buyers asking questions and writing up orders. Many times they wanted me to come to their stores to do promotions and sign CDs.

When Harald approached me, I read his badge, "Harald Wohlfahrt, Katie Wohlfahrt Christmas Stores, Rothenburg, Germany." He told me that he had twenty-five stores, but during the holidays he added seventy-five additional outlets, Kristkindle markets, all over Europe.

I had just been speaking with a client whose store was in a summer vacation resort. This client asked me to come to their store in July. When Harald and I discussed the possibility of performing at his biggest store, without thinking, I automatically asked him, "What is the busiest time of year for you?"

A strange look came over Harald's face and he said, "December. We are busiest in December because we have Christmas stores and Christmas is in December."

OMG, how am I ever going to recover from this? I howled inside my head, then I just had to laugh and explain about the conversation with the previous customer. I asked him if he could come back in a little while so we could discuss more of the details of me coming to Germany. He agreed, and when he returned we had a great conversation and really connected. He ordered 4,000 CDs on the condition that I would play at his store for twenty days in December.

Before saying goodbye, I asked him, "Where are you going next after Atlanta?"

"I have to fly to Minneapolis for a few days," he said.

"No kidding! I live in Minneapolis. You'll have to stay with us."

That was the beginning of a wonderful friendship.

And now back to the making of our film. Originally, the film was going to be twelve music videos of me, basically, playing Christmas songs in different locations in and around Rothenburg. There was no dialogue or story. We thought of it as just being something nice for people to watch during the holidays. But instead of making it a concert video, it would show off the beautiful landscape and medieval towns in Bavaria.

I'd been observing the beginning of the digital age back in 2002-03 as Napster, CD burners, iTunes, and iPods came on the scene. I figured it was only a matter of time before the role of music in our society would change completely. Would music survive?

While editing these twelve music videos, I got really bored of looking at myself on the screen. In the process of filmmaking, editing dialogue is normally quick and easy. The camera focuses on the character speaking, and once in awhile shows the character who is listening. To edit a five minute scene only takes about an hour. With music videos, it's a whole different story. A three minute song could take up to 16 hours to edit. Each song clip was a work of art and we had twelve of them to produce.

This is how I would describe the process. Imagine taking a million photographs and throwing them up in the air. After they randomly fall to the floor in a total mess, you need to look through all of them, one by one, to tell a story with a beginning, a middle and an end. It took more patience than I ever thought I had.

On top of that, I wanted to have double images. I chose a second ghost image under the main character to create a dreamy background. This multiplied the already arduous task. Slow motion, which had to be timed perfectly, was added for a dramatic, spiritual effect.

My decision to add a story was partly driven from being tired of looking at myself on the screen. I also thought this would give the film a better chance of being seen on television. We came up with the basic story of an Angel of Music and a little girl. Her grandfather would be telling her a story.

I envisioned that the Angel of Music came down to earth because there was no music left in the world. Harald didn't like the "no music left in the world" idea. But Sim had versed me well on conflict and even recommended Syd Field's book, *Screenplay*. I now had the basics of creating a screenplay. Displayed on page one of Field's book in giant letters is the statement, "Every film is about conflict."

So conflict was introduced into the movie. Unfortunately, now we had conflict between Harald and me that continued for months. "I want a nice family holiday movie with no conflict. It is a movie for Christmastime. Who wants conflict at Christmas?" He had a good point, but this was going against everything I had learned.

We filmed from January through March—only on

the coldest days. I was freezing out there, and my outfit for the film was not the warmest clothing. Thank God for the sheepskin shoe liners I'd purchased.

Harald was in one scene taking a picture with a Polaroid camera of the boy and me. We had to shoot that scene at least thirty times because his camera wouldn't work. It kept freezing up, and Harald ended up getting a terrible ear infection. He had to have his head wrapped completely in gauze at the hospital.

My life was perpetual jetlag, spending two weeks in Germany filming or editing, and then two weeks in America doing shows and seeing my family. I was back and forth for seven months. It had started off being fun, but it was getting exhausting.

Halfway through the filming, Harald called me to say that we had to decide why the Angel of Music came to the little boy. We were still in conflict and couldn't agree on what the actual conflict was in the film.

"Under no condition will there not be music in our town of Rothenburg," he said. "I am on the town board of directors, and they will not allow a film to be made that looks like something is wrong with our town."

"But it's only a movie and there would be no music anywhere else in the world either," I said.

"No way."

"There needs to be an important obstacle so there's a reason for the Angel to come help the boy," I said.

We were at an impasse. In my mind's eye I could see Harald arguing with me from Germany with his head all wrapped up in gauze because of his ear infection. Out of sheer frustration I said, "Then let's make the boy deaf. He wanted to be a musician, but fell in a lake, caught pneumonia, and lost his hearing. The Angel of Music needs to help him learn a lesson so he can get his hearing back."

I really didn't expect him to say, "OK," but he did.

That was it. And as luck would have it, Bush Lake was right behind my house in Bloomington. We found a cameraman and a stand-in boy to film the incident. The challenge was how to make the boy falling through the frozen ice look real. My cameraman used to live in Los Angeles and had worked with Steven Spielberg on one of his early films. He suggested we tie a rope to the boys feet, cut a hole in the ice and drop him in. (A camera man will do whatever it takes to get his shot.) There was no way I was going to be responsible for that.

In the end, we found a little stream that had frozen over, dropped a big rock on the thin ice, and the water from underneath came splashing up. We selected a scene we'd shot of the little boy falling and edited in the splash scene in slow motion. It looked real.

Now we had our conflict and we were all happy.

The lesson the little boy learned involved three golden keys. The angel had warned the boy to not go out onto the frozen lake, but he didn't listen. The boy needed to understand three golden keys of wisdom in order to learn his lesson and get his hearing back.

This is also the purpose of this book. Learning to listen to our Divine Inner Guidance. Incredible things happen when we listen to it, and more incredible things happen when we don't.

The boy's mom had taught him that any time you ask God for anything, if you add the three golden keys, you have a better chance of the wish being granted. The three golden keys was something I learned in Eckankar. If you wonder whether or not you should do something, first ask inwardly, "Is this true, is it necessary, is it kind?"

This was the foundation of the boy getting his hearing back, so I'd written this line into the story many times. The rest of the team started giving me a hard time about this, and they eventually hired another writer just to argue with me. Ahhh, more conflict. Actually, there was even more conflict going on behind the scenes than there was in the film, but that's another story to be told another time.

I meditated on the three golden keys and asked inwardly if I should fight to keep them in the film. I really didn't want to make the film without them. I felt strongly that it was a chance for me to share how important it is to listen to our own inner guidance. I asked God to give me a sign.

I had a little break before my next trip back to Germany. Since I'd been traveling so much and had so little time with my family, I took Emma to England for a few days. A friend who worked for the London Philharmonic Orchestra arranged for us to get two free concert tickets. We arrived at the hall, and in the lobby was a brochure stand displaying the many different things to see and do in London. We randomly picked out a bunch, I put them in my coat pocket, and then went into the concert.

The next thing I knew I was waking up to the sound of a lot of clapping. I asked Emma, "Why is everyone clapping after the first song?"

"The concert is over," she replied. "You slept through the whole thing and people are leaving now." Jetlag.

We enjoyed a few fun-filled days in London, then Emma flew back to the States. I went on to Germany. The issue of the golden keys was the next obstacle we had to tackle. Again, I surrendered the situation inwardly asking God for guidance.

My intuition directed me to look inside my coat pocket. The brochures I picked up a few days earlier were still there. A yellow brochure on top read, "The Society of the Golden Keys." This brochure was created by the concierges of London who became known as "The Society of the Golden Keys."

Concierges sometimes have difficult clients staying at their hotels and are given almost impossible missions to make them happy and get their job done. Through their creativity and their network of friends, they always found a way to do the almost-impossible. Making my first film in another country in two languages was an almost-impossible task for me as well.

When I arrived in Germany, a meeting was already scheduled to discuss the three golden keys in the film. I sat down and told them, "I asked God for direction and guidance about this. On the way here I found this brochure in my pocket." I held up the yellow brochure with "The Society of the Golden Keys" written on top. The discussion was over and not a word was said about it afterwards.

In the end, we finished our film. People of all ages have loved it and it's become a holiday tradition for many families. Harald and I are still great friends and we try to keep our conflicts to a minimum.

To view an excerpt from David's video *Village of Dreams*, enter **http://www. DavidYoungMusic.com/video/webCommercial.wmv** in your browser.

24

Noah's Basement

*E*mma and I bought an amazing house in an exclusive Bloomington neighborhood, and I became stepdad to Emma's two daughters. One of them had a biological dad who was easy to get along with, but the other dad was not. He vowed to ruin any chance for Emma's happiness in life.

He was a six foot body builder, big as a refrigerator, with a three-page police record. He broke into Emma's garage, got my phone number off of a UPS package, and threatened to kill me. He was the most deadly man I had ever met in my life. Eventually it became necessary to take out a restraining order against him.

He was a born-again Christian and left this message on my cell phone, "David, this is Goliath. You better fill your pockets with rocks, because I am coming to kill you." I'd been born into a Jewish family, and although I hadn't practiced Judaism after my bar-mitzvah and didn't know that much about the Old

Testament, I did know Goliath was killed by David in the Bible. What an odd thing for him to say.

Eventually all of his negative energy backfired. He lost his house, his driver's license, and spent all of his money on lawyers trying to attack us.

My career was at its peak when we bought the beautiful 5,000 square foot house in the expensive suburbs. The week after we moved in, our lovely neighbors left a note in the mailbox while I was out of town. The note read, "The garbage cans are supposed to be brought back up to the house no more than one hour after they are emptied by the garbage men. And a few of the lights on your house are burned out and must be replaced." The letter wasn't signed.

This set the tone for the whole time we lived there. If it wasn't one thing, it was another. You can choose your house, but you can't choose your neighbors. I was trying so hard not to let circumstances ruin life in my dream house.

The crazy dad moved within five blocks of us. My ex-wife Bridget, who I hadn't spoken to in years, decided to buy a house three doors down from us on the same cul-de-sac. The back of our houses faced each other. The day after she moved in, she told Annaliise she was forbidden to visit us.

Have you ever heard the saying, "When you get what you wanted, it's not always what you want?"

I started thinking about all of these negative things

happening at this new place and wondered, "Is this worth all the hassle?" We had bought the house for $600,000, and after I had the basement finished, it was worth $750,000. If we'd sold the house at that point, we could have paid cash for a smaller house in a less affluent neighborhood with the equity.

However, Emma was gun-shy. She moved eight times in seven years to get away from the maniac dad, so she didn't want to move again. I had also promised her before we moved in that we would stay there until the kids graduated high school.

I did ask her, "What happens if God tells us to move?" "I'm still not moving," she said. That's how adamant she was.

This was 2002-03, and the economy was still doing well. Everyone was making tons of money in the stock market and real estate was booming. Houses on my street were being sold for over $1,000,000. I had 1,500 gift stores buying music from me every month and life was grand.

At first I'd thought that all of the bad experiences in the new house were just testing me, but after awhile I started looking at it from a different perspective. Was something I couldn't see brewing going to make our wonderful house worthless in the future? Was it possible that Spirit was giving us these negative experiences to get us to move?

I recalled a talk my spiritual teacher had given

the previous year where he said we were "living in a golden age." I had the History Channel on one day and heard the narrator saying, "Every golden age is followed by a decline and then an age of rebuilding." Had my teacher been giving me a clue about what was to come?

Time moved along and I was still traveling all over the country almost every weekend. From that unique vantage point, I began to see the economy was starting to falter years before CNN talked about it.

There were a few reasons behind the changes. Smaller Main Street stores I sold to were being affected by the big box stores. It grew increasingly difficult for them to compete. How could a buyer with one store survive against a conglomerate with the buying power of 2,000 to 4,000 stores? The wholesale price of my CDs was $9.25. CDs in Walmart and Target were sold retail for only $9.99. In order to sell at lower prices, more wholesale products were being made overseas.

For 100 years, the basic rule of thumb in retail was called 'keystoning,' which meant the store bought products wholesale for $5 and sold them for $10. The retail price was double the wholesale price. That was becoming history. How could manufacturers in the U.S. compete with those in Asia where the hourly wage was $.25 instead of $12-$20 an hour?

Divine Inner Guidance, plus my common sense, told me that our economy was going to fail. Scary numbers of American manufacturing jobs were being shipped overseas. Once these workers lost their jobs, without any new jobs or means to support themselves, they would eventually lose their homes. When enough of them lost their homes, the banks that held their mortgages would be affected. In chess, when enough of the pawns in the game are lost, then the bigger pieces are exposed. Eventually middle management jobs would be sent overseas, jeopardizing the middle class.

I called my stock broker. I explained to him what I saw going on and what I feared was going to happen. He laughed at me. I held off.

The more I talked to Emma about it, the crazier she thought I was. Her successful friends in business would say, "Isn't David a spiritual man? How spiritual can he be with such a negative attitude about everything?"

I felt like Noah in the Bible. No one listened to me.

When Emma lost her great job, I wanted to rent out the 1,300 square foot, three-bedroom basement to help pay the $4,000 a month mortgage. My snooty neighbors had a fit and went to the city to try to stop it.

We were able to successfully rent it, though, and the first renter's name was Dave. He had a daughter named Brooklyn. An interesting coincidence. One of my neighbors actually screamed at him while he was pulling out of the driveway in his car, "You're just a renter!" But Dave stuck it out for six months, then when he got his life back on track, moved back in with his wife.

Our second tenant was Noah. It's funny that I'd been saying how I felt like Noah in the Bible. And now there was a Noah living in the basement of my house? How much closer can you get?

One morning soon after, I got a clear message from Divine Inner Guidance during my meditation to get my money out of the stock market the next time I heard it go up. Twenty minutes later I got in my car to drive to the studio when the news came blaring on. I never listened to the news, but somehow my radio had been tuned to NPR. The newscaster said, "The stock market has just gone up 100 points." That was my sign.

I called my stock broker in California and said, "I don't care if you laugh at me all day long, I want to get everything out of the stock market immediately!"

I was so adamant, he didn't argue with me. If I couldn't sell my house, I at least wanted to make sure I didn't lose everything should my gut feeling about the economy be right.

Two months later the stock market crashed. When I called my broker to check my account, he said I was the only one of his 200 clients that saw it coming and protected himself.

By the time I was finally able to convince Emma to sell the house, it was already too late. No buyers were looking for an expensive house like ours. The pressure of me having to travel to shows constantly, along with her being unemployed for so long, took its toll on us as well. Our relationship ended. The house went back to the bank and we lost our equity of over $400,000.

A few weeks after our breakup, I was at a big art festival in Ann Arbor, Michigan. I stopped by a concert hall while walking through downtown and discovered that Billy Dean, a friend of mine, would be performing the following Sunday. Billy won a Grammy for Best New Country Artist and sold millions of albums. I texted him to say that I was going to be in Ann Arbor for his concert and offered to play with him. He liked the idea.

I played the whole concert with him. It sounded like a Native American flute player accompany a country singer with an acoustic guitar. The crowd loved it. I guess I forgot to tell you the name of the venue. It was called "The Ark."

The following week in Chicago in 95-degree heat, I didn't get to a hotel until midnight. I was exhausted. The hotel clerk took my credit card and checked me in but said, "I'm sorry. I can't give you a key for your room right now. Our room key maker just broke. I'm afraid you'll have to wait here in the lobby until it gets fixed." Divine Inner Guidance nudged me to stay calm and wait.

There was nothing for me to do except sit there on the couch and look at the front door as people walked in and out. Ten minutes went by and a guy walked in who looked vaguely familiar. As he got closer, I realized that he was my friend who had played drums on ten of my CDs in Minneapolis!

He gave me a big hug and asked, "So what brings you here?"

"Oh, I'm just down here doing a show," I replied. "How about you?"

"I just finished playing a concert at Ravinia, the big outdoor venue, with my band, the BoDeans."

I did not have a chance to say goodbye to him when I left Minneapolis. Now we were staying at the same hotel. If I had received my room key at check-in, I would have gone up to my room to sleep and would never have known he was there.

He sat down next to me on the couch to chat just as the clerk brought over my key. The machine was suddenly fixed, but I stayed with my friend and we talked for the next hour. I guess I forgot to tell you what his name was. Noah.

Afterthought: The only thing missing in the story I just told was the flood. Back in the Bible, Noah is warned of an impending flood. I realized that our house had flooded three times when I wanted to sell it!

25

The Master's Helper

*L*ife in New Jersey was not suiting me. It was great to be closer to my family, but I was used to having so many friends in Minneapolis. Besides missing a woman in my life, going out to meet people in a big unfriendly city was like starting my life over from scratch.

The worst part was going to restaurants by myself day after day, night after night. It wore me down and made me feel bad about myself. Most women I know say they order takeout because they never eat in a restaurant alone. During my travels, I've had many wonderful, enjoyable experiences, but that month was just rugged.

While driving in my car during that time, I received a difficult phone call from my Los Angeles friend, Lisa Solana. Lisa had just suffered the loss of her father, plus she was in the middle of a custody battle over her two kids. She was hysterical. I tried to be supportive and said, "Your father's in a better place now," but I don't know how convincing I was. I was still wrapped up with the piles of problems in my own life.

I sat in my parked car asking God, "Is there any peace or happiness for me or anyone I know? I feel so displaced. I need a friend!"

It was about 6:00 p.m. and my stomach growled, letting me know it was time to eat. Another solo dinner was the last thing I wanted. I drove to the first sushi restaurant I could find and went inside. All of the tables were filled with smiling couples and happy families enjoying their meals. I walked to the empty sushi bar to sit down by myself.

I ordered from the sushi chef, trying to make small talk. However, he was Asian and couldn't speak English very well, so the conversation was kind of short. Then a guy about my age, wearing a Yankees cap and talking on his cell phone, sat down a few seats away from me. I thought to myself, "As soon as this guy gets off the phone, I'm talking to him!"

As soon as he hung up, I said, "Hi, my name is David, and I don't know anyone around here."

"Chris Solano," he said smiling. "I just moved to the area about a month ago, and I don't know anyone around here either."

During the conversation he told me his father had just passed away and that he was doing the best he could to adjust. Since I'd just gotten off the phone with my friend whose father had just passed away—and whose last name was Solana—it felt like something was lining up.

We talked about life, death, and spirituality.

"We all have a Soul," I said, "and sometimes we get a gut feeling or a knowingness. That is God directing us to be where we need to be. I call it Divine Inner Guidance."

"I know exactly what you're talking about," Chris said enthusiastically. "I wanted to go to another restaurant tonight, but I felt like there was a force pulling me to drive to this sushi bar.

"Once I got here, I sat down at a table in the back by myself. But, you know, that same force kept pushing me to come sit up here. I guess that's why I'm sitting next to you right now. I'm glad I did. I could really use a friend to talk to right now."

I reached out my hand and said, "We're friends."

Amazing how, when I needed a friend myself, God connected us at that sushi restaurant.

The conversation led to the subject of meditation. "I've been practicing for twenty-eight years," I told him.

"I really think I need to start meditating to find peace with all this change happening in my life," he said.

"I'd be glad to show you a technique after dinner," I said.

We paid our bills, and when we left the restaurant, I discovered that his white van was parked next to my car. The van was filled with construction equipment in the back. Chris was a handyman and his company name was painted in big letters on the van's side panel, "The Master's Helper."

His logo was right underneath the lettering. It was a rendition of the famous Michelangelo picture with God's hand reaching over to touch the hand of Man. My favorite painting.

"I use the word 'HU' as a mantra in contemplation," I explained. Then I taught him how to sing it and we started singing it together. We must have meditated for twenty minutes, and a beautiful sense of peace permeated the van.

Afterwards, he said, "I feel much better than I did before dinner."

So did I.

There's a saying that goes like this;

"If you want love in your life, then give love.

If you want friendship in your life, then be a friend.

If you want to see change in the world, then be the change."

26

Avoiding Conflict—After You?

Some shows I travel to are heaven on earth;
successful, nice people, appreciative comments on my
music, and so on. Other times, because of various
obstacles or bad weather, it's just the opposite.

Guess which one this story is about?

Five days of yucky, cold, November weather at
an outdoor show in Bentonville, Arkansas, and the
fact that I was ready to head home after the first day,
began to put me in a mood. Add to that the other fact
that the only flight I could book home left before the
end of the show.

Consequently, I had to track down someone with
the show to watch my booth for the last few hours,
pack up all my stuff, and then ship it to myself. It
rained buckets that last day, and I was not a happy
camper by the time I left the show.

On the way to the airport I got lost, so I didn't have

time to fill up the tank. As a result, when I dropped off my rental car I was charged extra for gas. Get the picture? More fuel on the fire.

I had to run to my gate and the plane was already boarding. As I was got my ticket ready to hand to the gate attendant, an older man cut in front of me and handed the attendant his boarding pass. I couldn't believe it! In all my years of travel, that was the rudest thing I'd ever experienced.

Once he passed through the gate, I quickly handed the attendant my ticket. I was so pissed, I fast-walked to pass him and got on the plane ahead of him. I shot him a dirty look as I walked by. (This probably isn't the kind of behavior you'd expect from the spiritual flute man, is it? Well, even the flute man has a bad day, LOL.)

So I boarded the plane to Detroit for the two-hour flight, the first leg of my trip home where I would transfer to Minneapolis. I settled into seat 2A. What a day! I saw the rude man board and walk to the back the plane. *Thank God he isn't sitting next to me!* I thought.

When boarding was almost completed, the last passenger came on and walked to my seat. Looking at the seat number on his ticket, he said kindly, "Excuse me, but I think you are sitting in my seat." He showed me his ticket which did show he was in 2A. I pulled out my ticket. It also read seat 2A.

We called a flight attendant, and she discovered that my boarding pass was for my next flight. I was supposed to be sitting in 12D. Even before I got out of my seat, I knew where Spirit was sending me.

Yes, I walked to the back of the small plane to the empty seat next to the guy who cut me off. We looked at each other in disbelief. Our facial expressions said, "Can you believe that we have to sit next to each other?"

My seat was next to the window, and my body language couldn't have been any clearer. If I'd been any closer to the window, I would have been on the other side of it.

The plane took off. Shortly after the flight attendant came around offering drinks.

"Chips, please," I said, taking $2.00 out of my pocket. I reached toward her with money in hand, but she was just beyond reach. Then, the man next to me gently took my $2.00 and handed it over to her for me. A kind gesture.

"Thank you," I said, surprised.

That started a conversation with him. I was amazed at what an enjoyable person he was. After some small talk, I asked him, "Where are you from?"

"Strongville, Ohio," he answered.

"No kidding, my older brother lives ten minutes

away from you in Ashland!" I said. "What a small world!"

Soon we were telling jokes to each other and having a blast. The flight attendant must have thought we'd always been best friends when she came by to pick up my empty wrapper.

There was such a nice vibe between us that I actually started to wonder if the "cut off" thing had happened at all. Did I create the whole thing in my head? Was my day so crummy that I transferred my bad feelings onto this nice man?

I wondered if I should ask him about it. If I did bring it up, and if he hadn't cut me off, I'd look silly. If I didn't ask him, I'd never really know whether I'd made up the whole conflict. Should I just forget it and let it go?

We chatted for the next half hour as I went back and forth in my head, Should I or shouldn't I?

When the pilot came on the intercom to say we'd be landing in about twenty minutes, I couldn't stand the mystery anymore. I couldn't let it go.

As courteously as I could, I asked, "You know it's been such a pleasure talking with you during the flight. But there's something I've been wanting to ask you," I hesitated.

"Yes?" he asked.

"Well, when we were boarding the plane at the

gate, it really seemed like you cut right in front of me. Now that we've been talking for the last two hours, I can't imagine you actually doing something like that. So I wanted to ask you about it."

The tone of his answer was genuine and courteous, "Nooo. Really? Oh my, I would never do that. I'm so sorry that you felt that way."

Can you imagine? What in the world happened back there? I shook my head. At least I had my question answered. I finally felt relief.

Since we were sitting in the back, even after the plane had landed, we had a long wait before all the other passengers deplaned. Finally our turn came, and as we stood up, he said, "It was nice talking to you, and I have something to tell you, too." His face cracked a smile.

"I did cut you off at the gate back there. But I'm really sorry!" The two of us burst out laughing!

He'd come clean, and I wasn't crazy after all. We walked off the plane with big smiles on our faces, joking around and chuckling.

Each of our transfer flights were on the opposite side of the Detroit airport, so we had quite a ways to walk to catch the tram. We stopped for a bite to eat, then continued on.

When we neared our departure gates, there was one moving walkway left. He stepped aside, swooped his hand in slow motion towards the moving walkway, and gestured me to go first.

"After you?" he said politely.

We cracked up, said goodbye, and went our separate ways. Conflict resolved.

27

Channeling George

*E*mma and I had separated in July, 2010 just before our nine year anniversary. Since I was leaving Minneapolis, my band Namasté was breaking up. I put so much time and energy into that project, and I swore that I would never write another song with words again. I needed to focus on my instrumental career and get serious because of the economy and everything that was going on in the music business with iTunes and downloading.

While I was driving across the country to move back to the East Coast, for some reason I kept listening to the George Harrison song, "Within You Without You" from *Sgt. Pepper's Lonely Hearts Club Band*. I'd hit the repeat button over and over for at least two hours each day. It was a peculiar thing. This song has a sitar on it and sounds very East Indian. Around this time I had a dream with George Harrison where I was late for a rehearsal and he was very serious. I didn't make too much of the dream.

I was a little too young to be a Beatles fan. I enjoyed hearing them on the radio and respected them, of course, but I had never learned any of their songs note-for-note on the guitar like I had with Led Zeppelin, Bad Company, and Pink Floyd. Oddly enough, between playing for Sir Paul, becoming friends with May Pang (John Lennon's girlfriend), and working with drummer Rich Schlosser (who played with Ringo Starr), I had more experiences in one way or another with the Beatles than any other group.

When I finally got to New York, I reconnected with an old friend who I hadn't seen in twenty-five years. He had found me on Facebook. When I got to his house, much to my surprise, the DVD of The Concert for Bangladesh was sitting on his TV set. I couldn't believe the coincidence. This was the benefit concert that George Harrison organized to raise money for the starving people of Bangladesh, Pakistan. I asked if we could watch it. We did and for the first time, I got a peek at the kind of man George Harrison was.

Later on that day, I drove back to New Jersey to see my mom and get ready to drive about four hours south to an art show in Baltimore. A taxi picked me up at my mom's in Cliffside Park, New Jersey, right across the river from Manhattan, and drove me 90 miles south to Princeton. I was carpooling with an artist friend who was driving to the same festival. In eighteen years of doing shows, I had never done this before.

When all of my CDs and sound system were loaded

into my friend's van, I jumped into the passenger seat. Sitting on his dashboard was a cassette tape of *The Concert for Bangladesh!*

"What is that doing here?" I blurted.

"I just took it out of an old box stored in my attic," he said. "I was at the concert in 1971 at Madison Square Garden, and I still have the two ticket stubs that I paid only $5.50 for."

Something was going on. It felt like a stirring inside me.

Two months later, I moved to a northern Philadelphia suburb close to Princeton and was introduced to a woman named Z while playing football with some friends. We had a really nice connection. She was also a yoga instructor, which is something I really enjoy as well. When I met her little daughter Zarina, I instantly bonded with her. She also looked just like one of Emma's daughters. Everything was falling into place, and I started having feelings for Z.

On our third date at a coffee shop, she asked me what the highlight of my career was, so I told her about playing for Paul McCartney. Then she told me that George Harrison used to babysit her as a kid! Obviously, I asked her how this came about, and she explained that her mom had met George at an ashram in the late 60s where they were both studying yoga and meditation. When her mom and dad separated, her mom and George started dating. After George fell in love with her mom, he moved both of them to England, and she grew up in the castle where he wrote the song "Here Comes The Sun." This was connecting the dots. It seemed like there was a reason for all of the bizarre coincidences that had occurred a few months earlier.

George's situation with her mom was parallel to mine with Z. We also had a few things in common. George had dark hair and dark eyes, sang and played guitar, practiced meditation and yoga and wrote songs with a universal message. We also shared the experience of adopting daughters, since I had adopted Emma's daughters.

Z was a yoga instructor, so I gave her some of my instrumental music that she enjoyed using in her classes. She had a vegetable garden in her back yard and made the most incredible vegetable barley soup ever. She agreed to give me free soup until 2015 in return for the CDs.

There was one problem though. Her heart had been broken four times in four years, so she was afraid to get hurt again. Each time we'd start to get too close, she would run away, and by that time I'd feel put out. Then after a few weeks I'd start to get over it, but then it was time for me to get more soup, which started the whole thing all over again.

Z had insomnia, which must have been contagious, because I got it as well. The only thing I could think to do in the middle of the night was write songs for her. It was getting out of control. I'd wake up at 3:00 a.m. and anything I would think of to say to her instantly turned into another song. I'd record it on my little tape deck, fall back asleep, and then in the morning I'd play it back and finish it. At 9:00 a.m. I'd call the studio to book time for the afternoon. By evening, a new song was recorded at which time I'd drop a CD copy of it in her mailbox.

One night while I was sleepless in my bed, wondering about some unique lyrics I had written, George appeared and played guitar for me. I'd never experienced anything like that. The music he shared turned into the song "I'm Still Missing You." Then the next day in the studio while I was recording it, he appeared to me again as a beautiful light that lit up the room and hovered in front of me for six seconds.

The engineer/studio owner was a guitar collector with 150 old vintage guitars. I drove him crazy trying to get the right sound on that song and recorded 12 tracks of my guitars. But I still wasn't happy with it.

"I need something that sounds different than my guitar, something with more of a clean, bell tone," I told him.

He pulled out a very old guitar from a closet, put it on the floor in front of me and opened up the case.

"I've never seen one of those before," I said. "What is it?"

"It's a 1955 Gretch," he said.

"What's the name of this guitar?" I asked. "What's it called?"

"It's called the 'George Harrison model,'" he said. "It was the same guitar that George made famous in the Beatles except this one is three years older. George played a 1958."

I used it on "I'm Still Missing You," and it was perfect.

I wrote and recorded twenty-five songs in thirty days. I was out of control. The only way Z could really hear what I was trying to tell her was in my songs. She would listen to them all day long, but every time we started getting close, something would happen to sabotage us. We ended it the day before Thanksgiving, and I was wasted emotionally, especially since I had just ended a nine year relationship only five months before.

As I was thinking about the whirlwind I had just experienced, I realized that all of the songs told a story of what it's like to meet someone, like them, fall in love with them, fall in love with their daughter, and think it's going to happen. Then, it's not going to happen. Then, it looks like it's going to happen again. Then, it crashes again, and finally you give up. (Plus you're out of soup!)

As I looked in my bathroom mirror, a thought came to me. If I had to give a title to this story, I'd call it "Channeling George." Instantly, a peace came over me. I started writing the details down as a book. It's been a long process.

Shortly thereafter, I told this story to a psychic friend named Debi and played her the song "I'm Still Missing You."

"You probably think that you wrote this song for her," she said.

"Well, yes," I answered.

"I don't think that's it at all. George wrote this song through you so he could tell her from Heaven that he still loved her and that he was still missing her," Debi said.

That seemed to make a lot of sense. It felt like his energy was driving the whole thing, but it was confusing. I thought the whole experience was about George wanting me to be with her so she'd have a man she could finally trust.

I expected the experiences with him to stop, but a few weeks later he came to me again. It was one of the most powerful experiences of my life. The closest I can describe it is it felt like being electrocuted—but in a good way.

During a deep state of meditation not long after that, a dark haired woman came to me. She kissed me on the lips and then disappeared. A few months later she came to me again, this time swimming to me in a dream. She kissed me on the lips again and disappeared.

I felt like someone from my past was looking for me, but I didn't know what to do about it. I moved to Florida a few months later.

An old friend connected me with a woman who grew up one street away from me. I had a crush on her all through junior high school and high school. Her name was Vicky. She had long dark hair and she loved to swim. She worked in Hollywood, Florida, off Young Circle on Harrison Street.

She had been a painter years ago, and I found one of her unfinished paintings in the spare bedroom. It had six large triangles in light grey and dark grey. I knew something important was going to happen with this painting someday. Her apartment was nicely decorated, but she didn't have any art in her bedroom. We decided to go to a Bed Bath and Beyond to see if we could find something.

A medium-sized piece of art really caught my eye, but there was a three-inch crack in the canvas.

"I have to buy this," I told Vicky.

"But, David, it's damaged!"

"Look at the colors, Vicky. Look at the burgundy trees. Look how nicely the brown, gold and gray areas work together."

"Well, okay. I give."

We took the painting back to her apartment and hung it over her bed. It looked perfect. Then I had a thought.

"Vicky," I asked her. "Could I add those colors; burgundy, gold, and brown to your grey painting with the triangles?"

"I started that thing ten years ago," she said. "I don't care what you do with it."

I'd never painted before in my life, but after Vicky showed me where she kept her paints I painted for ten hours, putting it up and taking it down. Each time I thought it was done, she cleaned the brushes. That happened eight times. I'd changed the whole design, and by the time I was finished, there were only three small grey triangles left.

Two weeks later Vicky bought me a book on George Harrison's life and in it was a picture of him after *The Concert for Bangladesh*, wearing his favorite jacket. It was made of a fabric with the exact colors and design that I had painted. You can see the painting and his jacket on the back cover of this book. I haven't stopped painting since.

While at her apartment, I had another dream with George, and I was surprised to see him. I'd thought the only reason he'd come to me was because of Z. In *this* dream, though, he was really happy. He joked around with me for the first time. He told me how much he enjoyed playing tennis on soft grass. I had no idea people played tennis on grass. It seemed bizarre that he was telling me this. Then he disappeared.

By that time I was working on the story "Channeling George" again. My editor had made contact with an agent in Hollywood and sent him the synopsis. The agent wanted to meet with me, so I booked a flight to Los Angeles for two weeks later.

While I was in the airport walking past a magazine store, I spotted a large photo of George on the cover of *The Rolling Stone* September issue. I bought it to read as I waited for the plane to board. Part of the article was an interview with his wife, Olivia. There were numerous things in the article about him that I had experienced nine months earlier.

There was also a picture of him having a gas playing tennis with Bob Dylan!

Right under the picture, in bold, were the words, "Forever Young." For some reason, since I don't appear to be getting older, my closest friends call me "David Forever Young."

To listen to "I'm Still Missing You" and two other George Harrison inspired songs written and performed by David, go to **DavidYoungRocknSoul.com** and click on "Music."

28

How to Be in the Right Place at the Right Time

*W*e all want to be in the right place at the right time.

If you had a rewind button to see what was happening before the magical moments of your life—when things just went perfectly—this is probably what you would see.

First, a moment of calm, then a moment of stopping for a second, then a gentle nudge to do something that you followed. One minute, ten minutes, or an hour later, you ran into an old friend you hadn't seen in years or you met someone that became a great business contact. The point is that you followed your Divine Inner Guidance and something wonderful happened.

Sometimes this guidance makes logical sense and sometimes it doesn't. The trick is to learn to recognize it and follow it.

At times it's a survival tool for our protection. At other times it's a magical door to a gift that's waiting for us. Listening to our intuition makes our lives better.

So how do we get to that place where we experience more of it?

The more we start thinking about our Divine Inner Guidance, the easier it is to recognize it when it pops up.

Have you ever thought about buying a certain car and then afterward, wherever you went, you saw that car everywhere? That car always existed, but it wasn't until you put your attention on it that you realized it was everywhere.

Tens of millions of people have seen or read *The Secret* and *What The Bleep?* or watched Oprah on TV. Positive thinking and new thought is commonplace now. Why not try it if you've never done so before? What do you have to lose?

Here's how you can start.

When you wake up in the morning, before getting out of bed, take a moment to open yourself to the possibility that Whoever, Whatever created you actually cares about you. It cares about your well-being and happiness.

Then try to create a moment of stillness in your mind.

With as much sincerity as you can, say this inwardly: I am open to your guidance and direction—and I accept your help which will benefit me and those around me.

The more love you put into it, the more powerful will be the return. You can repeat this exercise as many times as you like throughout your day. The Universe gives us back what we put out.

If increasing your intuition is something really important to you, to step it up, you can repeat the exercise by saying it over and over inwardly.

You can write it on a Post-it note and put it on the dashboard of your car, your bathroom mirror, and / or on your computer screen.

Look at it like this. You could practice the guitar one hour a day for five years—or you could practice for five hours a day for one year. You'll arrive at the same result, depending on how much energy you put into it.

If you do yoga, you can sing OM for awhile and then start repeating the exercise inside yourself. Or you can sing HU, the word I meditate with—then start. Whatever makes you feel closer to the Being that created you is helpful.

This page is something you can reread over and over to remind yourself.

To download twelve MP3s of David's "Most Peaceful Songs," either capture the QR code with your mobile device or enter **http://tinyurl.com/7yxnwla** your browser.

Made in the USA
Charleston, SC
20 July 2012